T0286669

The New York Times

CROSSWORDS UNDER THE COVERS
75 Enjoyable Puzzles from the Pages of *The New York Times*

Edited by Will Shortz

ST. MARTIN'S GRIFFIN ❦ NEW YORK

All of the puzzles that appear in this work were originally published
in *The New York Times* from August 24, 2005, to November 18, 2005.
Copyright © 2005 by The New York Times Company.
All Rights Reserved. Reprinted by permission.

ISBN-13: 978-0-312-37044-2
ISBN-10: 0-312-37044-X

First Edition: July 2007

10 9 8 7 6 5 4 3 2 1

The New York Times

CROSSWORDS UNDER THE COVERS

ACROSS

1 The "C" of U.S.M.C.
6 Opinion tester
10 "That's enough!"
14 France's Joan ___
15 Samoa's capital
16 Spy Mata ___
17 City chief
18 Lady's escort
20 Bit of encouragement
22 Bent over
25 Frankie of the Four Seasons
26 Stephen King novel
30 Wide shoe width
31 "Farewell"
32 The WB rival
33 Old draft letters
34 Casino supervisor
38 Cambridge sch.
41 Stocking's end
42 "___ hooks" (box warning)
44 CPR giver
47 Antes
50 "Me, too"
52 Pixies
53 Hoodwink
57 On the way
58 Wrinkled citrus fruits
62 Barbara of "I Dream of Jeannie"
63 Cries of surprise
64 Poor
65 Georgia and Lithuania, once: Abbr.
66 Corduroy feature
67 One with a dish towel

DOWN

1 Dot follower
2 Son ___ gun
3 Bit of sunshine
4 Request a hand?
5 Barely gather together, as funds
6 Chinese temple
7 Dentist's request
8 ___ remover
9 Plaster backing
10 Queen of ___, biblical V.I.P.
11 Mexican dish
12 Soothsayer
13 Little finger
19 Impose, as a tax
21 President pro ___
22 Restful resorts
23 Kennedy and Turner
24 "Miss ___ Regrets"
27 Centers of Christmas wrapping paper
28 G.I.'s address
29 M.D.'s associates
35 Skater Midori
36 Wee one
37 Envelop
38 Competition with shot putters and hurdlers
39 As to, in legal memos
40 Use a Frisbee
43 Bee or wasp
44 Catches sight of
45 Piles
46 Rag
47 ___ colada
48 Infectious fly
49 Kind of financing, for short
51 Daybreaks
54 Plenty, to a poet
55 Fed. workplace watchdog
56 Six-stringed instrument
59 Hula hoop?
60 Suffix with chlor- or sulf-
61 Damascus' land: Abbr.

by Sarah Keller

2

ACROSS
1 Congregation leader
6 Noted movie terrier
10 Excellent, in slang
14 Columnist Goodman
15 Very top
16 Prefix in the airplane industry
17 Large antelope
18 Numbers game
19 A bit blue
20 False rumor about seafood?
23 Needle part
24 Whistle blower
25 "Delta of Venus" author
26 Barnyard sound
29 40¢ per fifth of a mile, in New York City?
32 Greek earth goddess: Var.
35 New Deal program, for short
36 C. S. Lewis's "The Chronicles of __"
37 It's trapped indoors
38 Finis
40 Polish border river
41 Protozoan
44 Preschooler
46 Guernsey, e.g., in the English Channel
47 Holy chicken?
50 Disco __, "The Simpsons" character
51 A Perón
52 Timberwolves' org.
53 Onetime United rival
56 Chic scavenger?
60 Usually unopened mail

62 Eisenhower's Korean counterpart
63 George Burns movie
64 St. __, spring break mecca
65 Evening on Mt. Etna
66 Mapquest offering
67 Parrots
68 Mince words?
69 "Fabulous!"

DOWN
1 Witherspoon of "Vanity Fair"
2 Put to rest, as fears
3 Proclaim loudly
4 Not stay rigid
5 A Gandhi
6 Rest awhile
7 Oil price-setting grp.
8 Lessee
9 Tony Blair, collegiately
10 Catherine who wed Henry VIII
11 Sweat absorbers
12 Parabola, essentially
13 Play (with)
21 Queue cue
22 Kournikova of tennis
27 Sharon of Israel
28 On __ (how pranks may be done)
29 Spud
30 __ Domingo
31 C-3PO, e.g., for short
32 Lens
33 Shoot for

34 Immunize
39 Conductor's cue, maybe
42 Shade of red
43 Unfavorable
45 Forbidden: Var.
48 Redeemed, as a check
49 Stubble removers
53 Advice to a base runner before leaving base
54 Penned
55 Viper
57 Iowa college town
58 Actress Garr
59 Mao colleague
60 Bathroom installation
61 Get-up-and-go

by Leonard Williams

ACROSS

1 Popular pens
5 No trouble
9 Stopped dead
14 Gray's subj.
15 It may be gray
16 Upscale wheels
17 Split (with)
19 Not straight
20 Old brand advertised by Bucky Beaver
21 Level
23 Devil's take?
24 N.L. cap stitching
25 Showing no pity
29 Minos' land
31 Status __
32 Actor Morales
34 Investigator, at times
37 Treated roughly
41 Names hidden in 17-, 25-, 51- and 65-Across (twice in the last of these)
44 Primitive fishing tool
45 "Awright!"
46 "Java" blower
47 Public works project
49 Kentucky Derby prize
51 "I can't find a thing to watch!"
56 Cable choice
59 Avian source of red meat
60 Come down hard
61 Radical Hoffman
63 Hawked items
65 Procedure for a burn victim, perhaps
68 Rush-hour subway action
69 Marketing intro?

70 It goes in the middle of the table
71 Deviated, in a way
72 Did too much
73 Breyers rival

DOWN

1 Amount from which to figure sale profit
2 Ham-fisted
3 Procession
4 British gun
5 Put away
6 "Exodus" hero
7 Take care of
8 Late name in Mideast politics
9 Eruptions
10 Emeritus: Abbr.
11 Rust, e.g.
12 Relatives of the Xhosa
13 __ Park, Colo.
18 Not turning up much
22 Shingle abbr.
26 Suffix with kitchen
27 Labor leader George
28 Can't abide
30 Mideast capital
32 Golfer called "the Big Easy"
33 Tree yield
35 Having four sharps
36 __ poker (bar game)
38 Pajama part
39 Boot one
40 Summer hrs.
42 Knocked around
43 Send off

48 Telephone trigram
50 Run producer
51 Breezily informative
52 City on the Missouri
53 "One L" author
54 Zest
55 Ticked off
57 Peachy-keen
58 Parisian thinkers?
62 Highlands hillside
64 Party time, maybe
66 __ du Diable
67 __ Brooks, 1950's–60's "Meet the Press" moderator

by Alan Arbesfeld

4

ACROSS

1 Spur on a climbing iron
5 Temple V.I.P.
10 Less than a one-star movie
14 Saragossa's river
15 Lake Geneva spa
16 Mishmash
17 Macedonian king to those who knew him when
20 Old-fashioned ingredient
21 Medieval merchants' guild
22 Dug up
23 Pitts of old Hollywood
24 Quantity: Abbr.
25 Czar to those who knew him when
33 Waters naturally
34 Summit
35 Bagel filler
36 Herr Bismarck
37 Store away
39 Be ominous
40 "___ the fields we go"
41 It's a long story
42 Fiddle with
43 Prussian king to those who knew him when
47 "Lady" preceder, often
48 Put up
49 Draconian
52 Aplomb
54 Wanted notice: Abbr.
57 Czarina to those who knew her when
60 Mosque V.I.P.
61 Use a soapbox
62 Kill
63 New York's Carnegie ___
64 Whimpered
65 1956 hotspot

DOWN

1 Reverse, e.g.
2 Well
3 Unfettered
4 Sexy lass
5 Go over and over
6 Way of approach
7 Brief lives
8 Stripped
9 Third line on a ballot: Abbr.
10 Kind of shark
11 "The Good Earth" heroine
12 Difficult place to walk
13 Hopalong Cassidy actor
18 "___ life!"
19 Commingle
23 Stoicism founder
24 Yemeni port
25 86 is a high one
26 Gormandizer
27 British chemical lab measurement
28 Like the corn god Yum Kax
29 Prefix with center
30 Minister's calling, with "the"
31 Bulldogger's venue
32 Use with effort
37 1939 co-star of Haley and Bolger
38 86 is a high one
39 Stain
41 Jumping garbage cans on a motorcycle, e.g.
42 Dolts
44 Moolah
45 Narcotic
46 Like some coins and salads
49 Lose traction
50 Far from risqué
51 Enumerator's ending
52 Indiana town where Cole Porter was born
53 Iridescent stone
54 Leigh Hunt's "___ Ben Adhem"
55 Dance exercise
56 German auto pioneer
58 Quaint dance
59 Yellow Pages displays

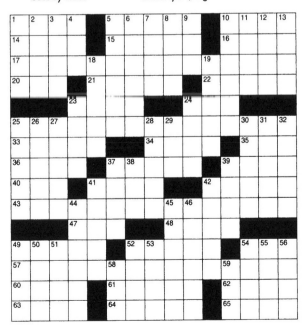

by Mel Taub

5

ACROSS

1 Test sites
5 D.H.'s pride
9 Without stinting
14 Paradise lost
15 "Rule, Britannia" composer
16 Frequent ticket office sight
17 Highflying industry
19 __ manual
20 Goal for a 112-pounder
22 Lover of Endymion, in myth
23 Klutz
24 "__ chic"
27 Like the Mau Maus
32 "Ugh!"
35 Top dog
37 Aces over eights, in poker, as illustrated by 17- & 20-Across and 54- & 60-Across
41 Carpenter's curve cutter
42 Born as
43 Like 90, compared to 85
44 San Juan de la __
47 Stephen of "Interview With the Vampire," 1994
49 Exotic vacation
54 25th anniversary gift
59 Presley's "Don't," not "I Beg of You"
60 Intensifies
61 Go-between
62 Indication of serious intent

63 Jam
64 Terrible twos, e.g.
65 Souvenir shop stock
66 Financial predicament

DOWN

1 Flips (through)
2 Jane Eyre's charge
3 Emerald or aquamarine
4 Senator from Maine
5 Kind of wit
6 Engage in fanfaronade
7 Mark of a ruler
8 Take care of
9 Water beds
10 Have to
11 Burn rubber, with "out"

12 Hook
13 Ouija board answer
18 On its way
21 Spoken for
25 Some sausage slices
26 Poison plant
28 Dance-drama with measured chants
29 10 jiao
30 Rice who wrote "Vittorio the Vampire"
31 Meeting point
32 Hankering
33 Half a train?
34 Had in stock
36 Bryn __
38 Morse bit
39 Weaken
40 Come to terms

45 Lexicographers' researches
46 Director/actor Braff of "Garden State"
48 Nirvana attainer
50 Sell for
51 Olds model
52 Kidney-related
53 "Don't you recognize this voice?!"
54 One may be heaved
55 Just think of it
56 Contact, say
57 Old Roman well
58 Benefit of clergy?
59 Easy mark

by Manny Nosowsky

6

ACROSS
1 Transgresses
5 Expostulate
10 "Now I get it," facetiously
14 Substance
15 Hard to read, perhaps
16 Stable shade
17 Way to stand by
18 Among those attending
20 Some rigging supporters
22 Gone bad
23 Radiator output
24 N.F.L. nail-biters
25 Guarantee
27 Spheres
31 Critical step in analysis
32 Richardson of Nixon's cabinet
33 Printed
34 In the capacity of
35 Cardinal features
39 Betty Boop trademark
44 Ump's cry
45 History book feature
46 Counselors' org.
47 Tacit
48 Coy expression
51 Verging on tears
54 Tension easer
56 It went through Memphis
57 "Juke Box Baby" singer
58 Clamorous
59 Counting method
60 N.F.L. coach known as "Ground Chuck"

61 Best dramatic actress Tony winner of 1948, 1978 and 1983
62 Yards on the ground, e.g.

DOWN
1 Spurt
2 Renovation
3 Pirate legend
4 Blocked
5 Yet undecided
6 Some summer residents
7 Gears up
8 New Eng. school
9 Dump
10 Alarm function
11 Appointed time
12 Response facilitator: Abbr.
13 Linear

19 Key card issuer
21 Second hand: Abbr.
25 Amanda's role on "Married . . . With Children"
26 Without __ (nonchalantly)
28 Fare after oral surgery, say
29 Do as Niobe did
30 Flat
36 Oration station
37 Water chestnut, e.g.
38 Eye
39 Infatuated with
40 Dope
41 Words of sympathy
42 Deck material
43 Business needs
48 Really warped

49 Screen symbol
50 Kind of pad
52 It runs down a limb
53 Noodge
55 Heavenly altar

by Joe DiPietro

ACROSS

1 Hopping good times
16 Has no pressing obligations
17 Placement pros
18 Former Solicitor General Ted
19 Nudges
20 O.T. book
21 Didn't cover for
25 Dig, for example
26 Modern rock genre
27 Restaurant seen in "Manhattan"
29 D.C. ballplayer
30 Get pickled
32 Union ___: Abbr.
34 "A pity"
35 Latin conjunction
37 Honeydew producer
41 Pulverizes, quickly
43 Base figure
45 Chassis
48 "Way to go!"
50 Washington's ___ Constitution Hall
51 Apple product
53 Woolly
54 Enzyme ending
55 Mapped sequences
57 Nips
59 Some nonproliferation treaty provisions
63 "Listen!"
64 Some picnic box contents

DOWN

1 Modern ad-hoc collections of computing devices
2 Source for the tune of "It's Now or Never"
3 Footwear in a 1959 Dodie Stevens hit
4 One-quintillionth: Prefix

5 Bad injury for a runner
6 Musician whose unusual first name means "ocean child"
7 Pommes frites topper
8 Deadly biter
9 Detachable, in a way
10 Fructose and others
11 Gov. Perry of Texas
12 Santa spotters?
13 Signals to start
14 Ods and endds
15 One of three in Byron's "She Walks in Beauty"
22 Word of encouragement
23 Communist land

24 Author of "Winter's Tales," 1942
28 Bug in a famous Dürer watercolor
31 Jerusalem ___
33 Make like
36 Already, in Arles
38 Tried
39 Considered one way
40 Promotes
42 Castle feature
44 Eyewash
45 Tara's foreman, in "Gone With the Wind"
46 Not dismissive of
47 Italian astronomer Giovanni Battista ___, after whom a comet is named
49 Object of Othello's jealousy

52 Saps
56 Philadelphia landmark since 1792
58 Locusts and wild honey, to John the Baptist
60 Yellow ribbon honoree: Abbr.
61 Wind dir.
62 Radar, e.g.: Abbr.

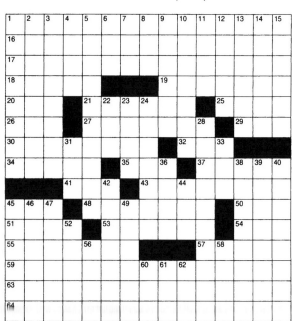

by Byron Walden

8

ACROSS

1 Mobile dining area
5 Quiet
9 Kind of surgery
14 Partly
15 "Put Your Head on My Shoulder" singer, 1959
16 Chocolate substitute
17 Strike
18 Shot's target, maybe
19 "Un Ballo in Maschera" aria
20 10's and 20's, e.g.
22 Rampaging
24 Literally, "high ground"
25 Subatomic particle
26 U.P.S. unit: Abbr.
27 French silk
29 Part of the Hindu trinity
31 Success on a slot machine
35 Preparations
39 "The Time Machine" race
40 It's not found within the four corners of this puzzle
41 Italian sweetie
42 "The Cosby Show" actress
44 X-__
45 Coconut fiber
46 Queue after Q
48 Perennial subj. of federal funding debates
50 Hair products
52 Next
57 Dignify
59 Washington landmark, with "the"
60 1986 Turner autobiography
61 Asian sea name
63 Cartoonist Walker
64 Writer of the "April Theses"
65 Red state
66 Moisturizer ingredient
67 Status-changing gift
68 "__ choice"
69 1929 literary character in San Francisco

DOWN

1 Mixer
2 Rising star
3 Lady friend in Italy
4 Fix, as a drive
5 Must
6 French individuals
7 Item between two poles
8 Former enemy capital
9 Deep-sea
10 Goal of a reading
11 It opened in 1825
12 Absent from
13 Possible result of a spicy meal
21 Certain race
23 Polite turndown
25 Impatient gift recipients
28 "__ a roll!"
30 Last of a Latin trio
31 Sportscaster Allen
32 Ayatollah __ Khamenei
33 Longtime NBC Symphony conductor
34 "Later"
36 Police staff: Abbr.
37 Afore
38 European carrier
40 Superman's father
43 How it all started, it's thought
44 Old TV host Allen
47 Shop worker
48 Singer with a 1978 #1 hit with Barbra Streisand
49 Log
51 Actor/comedian Denis
53 "Twenty Years After" author
54 __ Gay
55 Computer game format
56 Bag lady?
58 "Come __"
59 Prego rival
62 1990's Indian P.M.

by Kevan Choset

ACROSS

1 Gallery sign
8 It may lead to cooler heads
14 Stupid creep, slangily
16 Near-slave worker
17 Ape
18 Catalog
19 1993 A.L. batting champ John
20 Year the National University of Mexico was founded
22 Price abbr.
23 More likely to please
24 Newport rival
25 Tamiroff of "For Whom the Bell Tolls"
26 Suffix with social
27 Cornerstone word
28 Wool source
29 Author Rand
30 Sober
32 "Bwana Devil" was the first one
34 Happy-go-lucky
36 They may be turnoffs: Abbr.
39 Fine, in slapstick
40 Ballpark figs.
41 Unstable lepton
42 Temple part
43 Realizes
44 Approached rapidly
45 Cousin of a chickadee
46 Frank Sinatra's "Meet Me at the ___"
47 Fritz of the Chicago Symphony

48 Bag holder
50 Period of greatest success
52 Unrestrained parties
53 Look
54 Fake
55 Architects' work

DOWN

1 Unbreathable part of an atmosphere
2 Kind of TV
3 Come into one's own
4 Firewood measures
5 "It's all ___" ("I can't remember")
6 Installed
7 Tennessee River tributary

8 Announcement at the table
9 Start of a Mozart title
10 Daughter of Hyperion
11 Shipping charges?
12 Exposure
13 Loses one's cool
15 Site of a pitchers' lineup?
21 Easily-used people
24 Substantially (in)
25 Jai ___
27 Chrysler Building architect William Van ___
28 Charge
30 Seymour ___, the Father of Supercomputing
31 Pardner's mount
33 "___ goes"

34 Bygone haircut
35 Old armory stock
37 Adored
38 Causes of some domestic disturbances
41 Trader Vic invention
43 Au contraire
44 French royal called "Le Bon," and others
46 College figure
47 "Coriolanus" setting
49 More, musically
51 It comes in many vols.

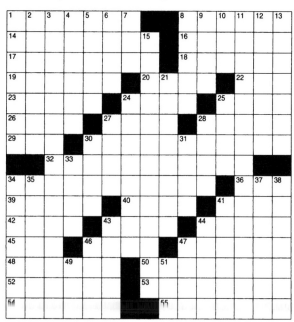

by Sherry O. Blackard

10

ACROSS

1. "Damn right!"
10. Contents of special lanterns
15. Like some loans
16. Get by force
17. Epitome of focus
18. London institution, with "The"
19. Tennis's U.S. Open is played on it: Abbr.
20. Great: Prefix
21. Common exfoliant ingredient
22. "The Erl-King," for one
24. Unisex winter apparel
26. Evening dress enhancer
27. Hints
29. Pet
30. Troubles
31. Alternative to sherbet
33. Nickname for Nantucket, because of its frequent fog, with "the"
35. Décolleté
37. Place for many pictures
40. Weather graphic
44. Short range?
45. Diamond stats
47. Extrapowerful
48. One working with a 23-Down: Abbr.
49. Mexican Indians
51. Disrespect
52. Derby parts
54. Route for Ben-Hur
56. Small house
57. Dear
58. Trapped

60. Children's author Danziger
61. Called for
62. How to cheat
63. Schedule checkers

DOWN

1. Holiday tradition
2. See 28-Down
3. Loser in a 1962 showdown with J.F.K.
4. Fuzzy flier
5. Cream
6. Marcus or Winfred of the N.F.L.
7. Losers in the Battle of Horseshoe Bend
8. Official fact finder

9. Mil. rank established by Cong. in 1862
10. Outfit
11. U.S. bank established in 1934, informally
12. Former German protectorate
13. Chilled
14. "Piece of cake!"
21. Giuliani adversary, once
23. Typing center
25. Publication concern: Abbr.
28. With 2-Down, handle perfectly, as a car
30. Novelist Huxley
32. Barn young
34. Recently: Abbr.
36. Ancient libertine

37. Daredevils
38. Abiding
39. Main man
41. Tall fern
42. Big Swedish export
43. Rolls
46. The Indians play them
49. Canine topper
50. Certain print
53. Spring place
55. 1969 Bond girl
58. First name in despotism
59. Finger-pointing, maybe

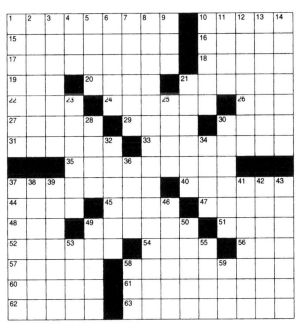

by Bob Peoples

ACROSS

1 N.B.A.'s O'Neal, informally
5 Armada parts
10 Shoots the breeze
14 Andean land
15 1992 and '96 third party candidate
16 Milky white gem
17 A couple of chips in the pot, say
18 Knight in shining __
19 Waiter's offering
20 California senator
23 Lucy's best friend
26 Water pitcher
27 Singer at Woodstock
31 Pharmacy weights
35 Historical period
36 Comet feature
37 Exactly right
38 Humorist Bennett who co-founded Random House
40 Long-billed marsh bird
42 Abhor
43 One-on-one teachers
45 Pitts of Hollywood
47 "Oh, my!"
48 Johanna __, author of "Heidi"
49 1972 Olympic swimming sensation
51 '60's civil rights org.
53 Came about
54 Comment when things are tough . . . or a title for this puzzle
60 Bulletin board fastener
61 Middle of a sink
62 Baby carriage

66 Tip-off
67 Slugger with 755 home runs
68 Prince Charles's sport
69 __ and haws
70 Tchaikovsky ballet roles
71 Puppy's cry

DOWN

1 Healthful retreat
2 Rooster's mate
3 Paintings and such
4 Where Montreal is
5 Wrangle
6 Parsley or bay leaf
7 "__ la Douce," 1963 film
8 More in need
9 Old mattress stuffing
10 Sin city of Genesis
11 Pinnacle
12 Cause of distress
13 "Dirty, rotten scoundrel," e.g.
21 Oodles
22 George Eliot's "Adam __"
23 Kicks out
24 Shredded
25 Robust
28 Mama of the Mamas and the Papas
29 Cousins, e.g.
30 Henry's fair lady
32 Slow symphonic movement
33 Sacred songs
34 "Bless you" preceder
37 Kneehole site
39 Abandons
41 What a golfer might shoot

44 Peel
46 Grp. with F-16's
49 Country singer Tim
50 Ivy League-ish
52 Musical endings
54 Measles symptom
55 Chronicle
56 Lowlife
57 __ Lee cakes
58 One guarding the steps of the New York Public Library
59 Rustic lodgings
63 Fish-to-be
64 Completely
65 Floor cleaner

by Lynn Lempel

12

ACROSS
1 Cavalier or Impala
6 N.B.A. star in the '96 film "Kazaam"
10 Predicament
14 Eagle's home
15 Hot-and-sour soup ingredient
16 Get misty-eyed
17 Fifth Amendment issue
20 Boat in "Jaws"
21 Guesstimate phrase
22 Church recesses
23 City on the Rhone
25 Gung-ho
26 Ulterior motive
31 To no ___ (fruitlessly)
32 Biblical flood insurance?
33 ___ vu
37 Congressional declaration
38 "Mr. Jock, TV quiz Ph.D., bags few lynx," for example
42 Wrigley Field player
43 Where pants may have a hole
45 Director Howard
46 Lyric poem
48 Australia was the first country to implement it
52 Billiard shots
55 Longtime host of "Scientific American Frontiers"
56 Cover story?
57 Bantu language
59 ___ Toys, maker of the Magic 8-Ball

63 Intelligence endeavor
66 Pirouette points
67 Like most graffiti: Abbr.
68 Flower part
69 "Provided that is the case . . ."
70 Man with a top hat and cane
71 College chief

DOWN
1 Mafia bigwig
2 Frau's partner
3 Rocker Clapton
4 "The Four Seasons" composer
5 Roll-call vote
6 Breastbones
7 Brewer's need
8 A young Michael Jackson had one

9 Quid pro ___
10 Acquired family member
11 Intrinsically
12 Like some cereals
13 Rendezvous
18 Tom or Jerry of "Tom and Jerry"
19 Cowpoke's bud
24 Canine plaint
25 44-Down singer
26 Peddle
27 Pavlov of Pavlov's dogs fame
28 "How ___ you?!"
29 Eric ___, 2004 Dodger All-Star pitcher
30 Blunder
34 E.P.A. concern: Abbr.
35 Unarmed combat
36 Help in a heist
39 Circle segments

40 Neither here ___ there
41 Lake ___, reservoir on the Colorado
44 1962 hit subtitled "That Kiss!"
47 45, e.g.
49 Qatari leader
50 "American Idol" display
51 Fuzzy image
52 Desert bloomers
53 Reserved
54 Tears apart
57 Basketball defense
58 Stratford-___-Avon
60 "Holy cow!"
61 Try to persuade
62 Exclusive
64 Put out, as a base runner
65 Egyptian snake

by Barry C. Silk

ACROSS

1 French cherubs
6 Fish often split for cooking
11 Field hospital sight
14 "Beavis and Butt-head" cartoon spinoff
15 Honky-tonk sight
16 Washington's ___ Stadium
17 Bullfight setting
18 Riverbank burrower
19 36-Across craft
20 About 4 million Americans, religiously
23 Elephant's weight, maybe
24 Other, in Madrid
25 Gutter site
28 How the sirens sang, in myth
31 Lobster's cousin
34 Mauna ___
35 Politician's goal
36 19-Across passengers
37 Pop artist whose name is an anagram of 20-Across
41 Low-tech missile
42 Affixes
43 Amniotic ___
44 Fast-paced sport
46 Certain drive-thru requirement
50 Chinese dynasty a thousand years ago
51 Greek cheese
53 Month of l'année
54 Like the most devout churchgoers and another anagram of 20-Across

59 Headhunter's big recruit, for short
61 Not express
62 Allots
63 Hairy hand
64 Tropical palm
65 Spring up
66 Mozart's home: Abbr.
67 Short-fused
68 Deli choices

DOWN

1 Doesn't stay the same
2 Taper
3 "Brighton Rock" novelist
4 Zwei halved
5 Swedish export
6 Poor, as coverage
7 One making references
8 Routines bad to be on
9 "Dedicated to the ___ Love"
10 "Dumb ___" (old comic)
11 Follower of Richard the Lion-Hearted
12 Popular insect repellent
13 Bout stopper, for short
21 ___ Griffith, 1999 W.N.B.A. M.V.P.
22 "What's ___?"
26 Dye holders
27 Masthead contents, briefly
29 Inventor Whitney
30 Demolish
32 50 Cent, e.g.
33 Starters
35 Method: Abbr.
37 Bringer of wine and flowers
38 Post-storm effects
39 Skyscrapers, e.g.
40 N.C. State is in it
41 Bedwear, for short
45 Subject of a guessing game
46 Having fun
47 Carson McCullers's Miss ___ Evans
48 Hardest to find
49 Slams
52 Put into law
55 Bed board
56 Burned up the highway
57 Biblical evictee
58 Days long past
59 Tax pro, for short
60 Water, in the Oise

by Andrea C. Michaels

ACROSS

1 Sight at St. Peter's
6 Appliance figs.
10 Come together
14 Titanic V.I.P.
15 A Mrs. Chaplin
16 End of the old switch
17 Lament on a washed-up celebrity's answering machine message?
20 Show without acting
21 Together
22 Two-time loser to D.D.E.
23 Something I can't use, but you can
24 Promise on a patient prosecutor's answering machine message?
32 Low-lying area
33 Bandleader Skinnay ___
34 Satum model
36 Part of the Gulf Coast: Abbr.
37 Igneous rocks
39 Comic Philips
40 Vet's old locale
41 Links legend, informally
42 Rama V's land
43 Advice on a fitness instructor's answering machine message?
47 One-pointers: Abbr.
48 A Beatle bride
49 Shine
52 Lousy
58 Instruction on a record executive's answering machine message?

60 Memo opener
61 So
62 Backs
63 Coal area
64 Many a Nintendo player
65 1983 flick "___ and the Cruisers"

DOWN

1 It's not much to show
2 "Woe ___!"
3 It held down the giant Enceladus, in myth
4 "You had your chance"
5 More chichi
6 Lacking meat, so to speak
7 Start of a suit
8 Duke, e.g.: Abbr.

9 Slump
10 Resort-goers
11 Cosmetics maker ___ Laszlo
12 Nut
13 Pitcher Derek, 2004 Red Sox World Series hero
18 Tiny, informally
19 Hector
23 Set down
24 Soviet Literature Nobelist Bunin
25 1980's–90's TV drama
26 Long-necked animal
27 Kind of question
28 Kind of personality
29 Empty, as rooms
30 Follower of cow, pig or horse
31 Pontius Pilate, e.g.

35 Biggest town on Norton Sound
37 More than a scrap
38 Canine pleas
42 Rushed
44 Assuming, hypothetically
45 A driver may sit on it
46 Put up with
49 Bush and Kerry, collegiately
50 Lawless role
51 Irene of "Fame"
52 Rushed
53 Record-setting
54 Smooth
55 In ___ way
56 Polo of "Meet the Fokkers"
57 European tongue
59 So far

by Ben Tausig

ACROSS

1 Aerie area
5 Axis leader
9 Floored
14 Celebratory dance
15 With 23-Across, winner of seven Oscars
16 French film award
17 They pop on planes
18 He surpassed Smith as the all-time winningest N.C.A.A. tournament coach
20 Totally
22 Much may go on behind them
23 See 15-Across
24 Food thickeners
26 Gillette alternative
28 News sources
32 Spanish "no son," translated
33 Bright circle?
34 It might follow a dot
35 "Follow my lead"
37 Picked teams, perhaps
39 "The significance being . . . ?"
40 Product in mint condition?
42 Hollywood's Hayek
43 It might result in an important decision
45 Rouen resident, e.g.
46 With 63-Across, domestic, e.g.
47 Good thing to have in competition
48 Larva place
51 Took a piece from?
55 Biblical beast
57 Tops
58 Tie-up
59 Class stopper
60 Set item
61 1946 Literature Nobelist
62 "O-o-oh"
63 See 46-Across

DOWN

1 Special creator?
2 Die laughing, so to speak
3 Ones given the shaft?
4 Carriers under city streets
5 "I'm very disappointed in you"
6 "Al ___ Lado Del Rio" (Best Song of 2004)
7 Time of extravagance and hedonism
8 Direct conclusion?
9 Malt alternative
10 State-of-the-art
11 Society: Abbr.
12 Boat trailer?
13 Thrower of the apple of discord
19 One of a famed family of entertainers
21 Parts of seven countries lie within it
25 Targets of some busts
26 Slain peacemaker
27 Snow White's poisoner
29 "Go on"
30 Problem for a horticulturist
31 Red Sea borderer
33 Kind of alphabet
36 Want
38 Spreadsheet software option
41 Victoria's Secret purchases
44 Collection agcy.
45 Parent company of Alpo, Friskies and Fancy Feast
48 Run . . . or ruin
49 Female suffix
50 Reading stops: Abbr.
52 Many a resort
53 Tautomeric form of vitamin C, e.g.
54 2005 portrayer of Wonka
56 Diamond stat.

by Kyle Mahowald

16

ACROSS
1 Blood: Prefix
5 Cynical comment
9 Flank
13 Popular whitener
14 Melba, e.g.
15 Singer at the Live Aid concert
16 Symbols of innocence
18 Auto pioneer Adam
19 Those who prefer suspense?
20 ___ provençale
21 Passed quickly
22 Candy manufacturer Harry
23 It's nonsense
26 1988 buyer of Motown Records
27 Like Mars nowadays
28 Uniform part
29 Old riddle: "What did Delaware?" Answer: "I don't know, but ___"
31 Event that didn't happen
38 Sharp
39 Shellac finish
40 Old English entertainment
43 1910's French avant-gardist
45 Big shot
46 Carry on
47 Fictional miner with heavy eyelids
49 1979 Fleetwood Mac hit
50 Writer, slangily
54 Pervasive quality
55 Hunters' decoys
56 Winged goddess

57 Wolf
58 Not to be missed
59 Pit
60 Suffix with super
61 Mortal Kombat maker

DOWN
1 Seasonal greeting
2 Christian denom.
3 N.Y.C. thoroughfare in the Rodgers and Hart song "Manhattan"
4 Beth's predecessor
5 "No opinion"
6 Why 31-Across didn't happen
7 Tip reducer
8 "Working Girl" girl
9 At a premium

10 One working with a crook
11 Edginess
12 Struck
13 Local govt. unit
17 Study, say
22 Wolf
23 Glittered
24 A pearly white
25 When some stores open
27 Publisher's pile: Abbr.
30 Letter opener
32 16
33 Beat, and how!
34 Swedish coin
35 Put away
36 Creature with many sharp teeth
37 Put down
40 Some fraternity members

41 Settlement in le Nouveau Monde
42 Butterfly, e.g.
44 Sports hero who wore #10
45 Specifically
47 Supercilious one
48 Characters of a certain type
50 2002 Literature Nobelist Kertész
51 Drain sound
52 Supermodel Benitez
53 18 through 20, in a run

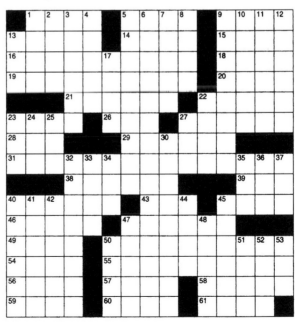

by David J. Kahn

ACROSS

1 British rule in India
4 Eject, as lava
8 Multigenerational tales
13 Cowboy boot feature
15 Read (over)
16 Trashy sort
17 Lowland
18 First-rate
19 With 67-Across, a whisker cutter
20 Dollar amount indicated on 55-Across
23 Sunshine State city
24 "That hurts!"
25 Gathers leaves
28 Mailing label words
33 "Stop yelling ___!"
36 Jazzy Fitzgerald
38 Lend ___ (listen)
39 Niceties following 29-Downs
42 Instant
43 Opposite of "ja"
44 Canadian gas brand
45 "Seriously, don't bother"
47 Mythical being with horns
49 Playing card dot
51 Gives the gas
55 Forms filled out for potential employers
61 Smell
62 Ignoring modern sensibilities, for short
63 Island of Napoleon's exile
64 Hysterical

65 Yards rushed, e.g.
66 "Hold it!"
67 See 19-Across
68 Nozzle site
69 Hwys.

DOWN

1 Replies to an invitation, briefly
2 Separately
3 Minty drink
4 Backup means for gaining entrance
5 Impoverished
6 Sea eagle
7 Full of dandelions, say
8 Summer headwear
9 ___ Sea, which is really a lake
10 Strip in the Mideast
11 Love god
12 Surprisingly lively
14 Letter often accompanying 55-Across
21 Flight board abbr.
22 Call for help
26 North Carolina's ___ University
27 Swings around
29 Helpful step for an employment seeker
30 Preceders of cues, alphabetically
31 Blackens
32 Approximately
33 Memo heading abbr.
34 "Comin' ___ the Rye"

35 Common street name
37 Inter ___
40 Not fall behind
41 Theater intermission
46 Plunge
48 "Is it soup ___?"
50 Luxurious
52 ___-powered
53 Ignored, as a bridge suit
54 Hurdles for H.S. juniors
55 Doorpost
56 Face-to-face exam
57 ___ fide
58 In the thick of
59 Wild about
60 Book auditors, for short

by Michael Shteyman

18

ACROSS
1 With the bow, in music
5 Dutch pottery city
10 Disney clownfish
14 Satirical Mort
15 Writer Zola
16 Plow team
17 Author Silverstein
18 Like some panels
19 Diamond complement
20 1994 Ethan Hawke movie
23 D.C. baseballer
24 Choler
25 Singers James and Jones
28 Nougat candies introduced in 1922
33 Milo of "Ulysses"
34 Luau strings
35 Run without moving
36 Like tumblers
40 Use an old phone
43 Ram's ma'am
44 Capital at 12,000 feet
48 "Monty Python" birds
52 Gaynor of "South Pacific"
53 Airline's home base
54 Teachers' org.
55 Some e-mailed news reports
60 Leopold's 1920's co-defendant
62 Cook in a wok, perhaps
63 Sweep's schmutz
65 Book after Proverbs: Abbr.
66 Tree with catkins
67 Heavy reading?
68 Siouan speaker
69 Rebellious years, often
70 Snick-or-___

DOWN
1 Chucklehead
2 Cheering section cheers
3 Fastest land animal
4 Spicy stew, or its pot
5 Hanker for
6 Is histrionic
7 Pad producer
8 Spare tire, so to speak
9 Dustin's "Tootsie" co-star
10 Hardly aboveboard
11 Used to be
12 Game pieces
13 Calorie count of some diet drinks
21 Purplish
22 Gumshoe
23 Sgt. or cpl.
26 Shoemaker's tool
27 Chicago-to-Miami dir.
29 Within reach, as a goal
30 Down the ___
31 River to the Volga
32 Tightrope walker's need
37 Stephen of "The Crying Game"
38 Have in hand
39 "Well, ___!"
40 Hoover, e.g.
41 "See ___ care!"
42 Erte forte
45 Seaplane float
46 "Totally cool!"
47 When doubled, sister of Eva
49 Early second-century year
50 Make less dingy
51 Boring tools
56 Aspiring J.D.'s exam
57 Where the Clintons met
58 Fellow, slangily
59 J.F.K. landers, once
60 Late July baby
61 When the Supreme Court reconvenes: Abbr.
64 Ball raiser

by Stella Daily and Bruce Venzke

ACROSS

1 Particular
5 Particular, for short
9 Data processing room
14 Looking up
15 Celestial bear
16 Geneva's river
17 Petri dish filler
18 Wife of Jacob
19 Give the slip to
20 What this puzzle has? (not really)
23 Give ___ to (prompt)
24 Stan who created Spider-Man
25 Thanksgiving side dish
28 In perfect formation
31 Mattress problem
34 Bubbling over
36 Neptune's realm
37 Essayist's alias
38 Like this puzzle? (not really)
42 Without a partner
43 Arthur Godfrey played it
44 Nobelist Bohr
45 A.A.R.P. members
46 Treated with contempt
49 Church ___
50 Liberal arts maj.
51 ___ about
53 What this puzzle is composed of? (not really)
61 Super success
62 Life of Riley
63 Yawn producer
64 Stroke of luck
65 Monopoly stack
66 "The very ___!"
67 Like a celebrity

68 Bronx/thonx rhymer
69 Grown-up eft

DOWN

1 Modern-day theocracy
2 Take-out
3 Biblical twin
4 Loy of filmdom
5 Element in gunpowder
6 Victimizer
7 Actor Morales
8 "High Hopes" lyricist
9 Aspiring doc's program
10 Daphnis's love
11 Boorish sort
12 "Me, myself ___"
13 Bone to pick
21 Stud declaration
22 Twinkle

25 Some two-masters
26 Can't take
27 Is dreamy
29 A tribe of Israel
30 "___-haw!"
31 Built for speed
32 Steward's beat
33 Like a windbag
35 Suffix with duct
37 QB Manning
39 New Mexico's state flower
40 Ref's declaration, for short
41 Provide funds for
46 In cubbyholes
47 Implements of western justice
48 Catch in a net
50 Anti-vampire tool
52 Maid Marian's man

53 Mutt's buddy, in the comics
54 Bruins' sch.
55 Ratty area
56 It's inert
57 Agent Scully
58 Hectored
59 Was in a no-win situation?
60 Candidate's goal

by David Elfman

ACROSS

1 Home free
5 Condescend
10 Beam intensely
14 Pristine plot
15 Caste member, say
16 Grimm opener
17 In one's Sunday finest
19 Stooge's laugh syllable
20 Union demand
21 Interrogate
23 Rush-hour hour
24 Flamenco guitarist Carlos
29 Antithesis: Abbr.
31 Like, with "to"
32 Swazi, e.g.
34 Old paper section
37 Carousing
39 Hank of Hollywood
41 Like just the draft of an e-mail
42 Violet variety
46 A.A.A. and B.B.B., e.g.
47 Biscotto flavoring
48 Jamison of the N.B.A.
50 In position
51 Opt not to charge, perhaps
53 Castigate
56 Sword parts
58 Aria sung by Renato
60 Burlesque show accessories
61 What a vertigo sufferer may wonder
66 Neighbor of the radius
67 Stomach
68 Radar unit?
69 Crane construction

70 In need of a muffler
71 Something to stage

DOWN

1 Retail giant
2 Two-time loser to Ike
3 Name of three popes
4 Some linemen
5 Any car, affectionately
6 Bard's contraction
7 Follower of add, slip or come
8 Horatian work
9 A little overweight
10 TV's Anderson
11 For even a minute more

12 Making a bust, maybe
13 Cry in cartoons
18 Riviera's San __
22 Follower of Meir and Shamir
25 "Venice Preserved" dramatist Thomas
26 Greatest possible
27 Before-long connection
28 Inspiration for Lennon's "Woman"
30 Tries to hole out
31 Toes' woes
33 Williams of "Happy Days"
34 15-Across rulers
35 Problem linked to CFC's
36 Papeete's people
38 Cocoon residents

40 Fumble-fingered
43 Cousin of a crow
44 Family member, for short
45 Training org.?
49 "That was close!"
52 Nile spanner
53 Coin of Qatar
54 "__ far far better thing . . .": Dickens
55 Far from reticent
57 D.A.-to-be's hurdle
59 Alternative to stairs
60 Hair style
62 "Deadwood" airer
63 Junior's junior
64 Parts of finan. portfolios
65 "What's the big idea?!"

by Frank Longo

ACROSS
1 Rafts
5 Maned grazer
15 Sharp
16 Disappointing course finish
17 Drive
18 It's not jotted down
19 Windbags
21 Ushered
22 Seat cover?
23 Without
24 Kind of bar
27 Marriage bond
28 Tidy sum
31 Spy tool, briefly
34 Lets go
35 Draft pick
36 Take for a ride
37 Opposite of hence
38 Opening statement?
42 They're counted in gyms
43 Diamond deals
44 Do major harm to
47 DuPont trademark
49 Billionaires and their families, e.g.
50 Magic was part of it
54 Asian appetizer
56 Moon surrounder
57 "No more Mr. Nice Guy!"
58 Plays for a sucker
59 Patter
60 Broken-off branch

DOWN
1 Evidence of an admission
2 Certain peer
3 It made it past sirens
4 Some crocks
5 Distaff
6 Apt to stay put
7 Imparts
8 Colon composition
9 Actress/model Mendes
10 He may carry your burdens
11 Cyclotron inventor __ Lawrence
12 Literary invention of Archilochus
13 Subbed
14 Nottingham is on it
20 Be hesitant
23 Curry of "Today"
24 Grp. concerned with lab safety?
25 Perch for an ibex
26 Home of the National Automobile Museum
27 Supporter of a proposal?
29 Adds to dishonestly
30 Y wearer
31 Coagulate
32 Architectural projection
33 1962 expansion team
36 Plant of the pink family
38 Keys on maps
39 Lummox
40 Cat burglar's need
41 Native to
42 Rhea, e.g.
44 Breaks in scores
45 Leader of the pack?
46 Like some bugs
47 Unfriendliness
48 Holdover
50 Trier trio
51 Naturalness
52 Blind jazz pianist Templeton
53 Just 'bout
55 Political inits.

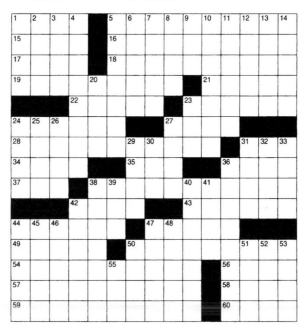

by Craig Kasper

22

ACROSS
1 Immodest Googling
11 Booted, say
15 "The Three Musketeers" actress, 1948
16 Geometric shapes
17 Reran
18 Threads
19 Narrow-sleeved garments
20 "Wow!"
21 Cornering challenges
22 New York college founded by Franciscans
24 Course error
26 ". . . __ the set of sun": "Macbeth"
27 Moray eel victims
29 Together
31 Wind or water
33 Ex-lax?
34 Soviet W.W. II foreign affairs commissar
38 Island with the volcano Mt. Liamuiga
40 Paris-born painter Tanguy
41 Subject of Drumnadrochit village observation
43 Abbreviated
45 Went boldly
50 Plug end
51 Shows a desire to get in
53 48-Down resident
54 Series about the firm McKenzie Brackman
56 Large predator

58 Subject of a museum in St. Petersburg, Fla.
59 Former Platte River dwellers
60 Deli offerings
62 Hat-tipper, say
63 Asceticism feature
64 Strategic W.W. I river
65 Exhibit artfulness

DOWN
1 Fort Bliss city
2 Like some victims of the Vandals
3 For anything
4 Declines
5 Mountain West conference player
6 Unrefined

7 Aristophanes drama, with "The"
8 Bedbound
9 Poverty
10 Bite preceder
11 Censor's list: Abbr.
12 Watched things
13 Get to go . . . or make go
14 Doesn't go along
21 Lyrical period
23 Ticked off, after "in"
25 Hoover's vice president
28 Like some transfers
30 "Lord, is __?": Matthew
32 Hints
34 Science dealing with fungi

35 Makes eggs, in a way
36 Much less
37 1942 F.D.R. creation
39 Teenager of old comics
42 Barren
44 Sound uncertain
46 Altered
47 Wood sorrel genus
48 Trinity River city
49 Stick on a key?
52 Mock
55 Science class: Abbr.
57 "__ quote . . ."
60 Sch. in Stillwater
61 Cartoon pooch

by Rich Norris

ACROSS

1 "Whew! The workweek's almost over!"
5 Ready for picking
9 Adjust
14 Indian princess
15 Disney's "__ and the Detectives"
16 Nonsocial type
17 Memo-heading abbr.
18 Alan Alda series
19 Weak and thin, as a voice
20 Chinese main dish
23 Veer sharply
24 Hymn-playing instruments
28 Actress __ Dawn Chong
29 Slight downturn
31 Trade
32 Wading bird
35 Unyielding
37 Santa __ winds
38 Reagan's tax policy, to detractors
41 Astern
42 Less polite
43 Emblem on an Indian pole
44 Dire prophecy
46 Frisbee or Slinky
47 Big mfr. of A.T.M.'s
48 Mailing a letter or picking up a quart of milk, e.g.
50 Hype
53 Holler upon walking in the front door
57 State bordering Canada for 45 miles
60 Japanese sashes

61 Wife of Osiris
62 Carries
63 Solomonlike
64 Pics from which to make more pics
65 "You should be embarrassed!"
66 Reply to "Shall we?"
67 Suffix with switch

DOWN

1 Streetcar
2 Los __, Calif.
3 Like a trailer behind a car
4 ID'd
5 Erase
6 Icon
7 Leaning tower site
8 1-to-12, gradewise

9 Place to exchange vows
10 Events
11 Raggedy __
12 Bic or Schaefer
13 Attempt
21 Rhetorician
22 Make a surprise visit
25 Expect
26 1930's vice president John __ Garner
27 Twitch
29 Rather risky
30 Composer Stravinsky
32 Escape, as detection
33 Attempt to get
34 Helicopter feature
35 Make over
36 E-business

39 Surpass
40 Narcotic pain reliever
45 Havoc
47 Squeak and squeal
49 Condemned's neckwear?
50 Raise
51 Doofus
52 Friend in a sombrero
54 Wolf's sound
55 Theater award
56 Bygone U.S. gasoline
57 The "I" in the answer to 1-Across
58 Dumbbell's cry
59 See __ glance

by Timothy Powell

24

ACROSS
1 Eller of "Oklahoma!," for one
5 Striped swimmer
9 Signs of boredom
14 Dagger of old
15 Folkie Guthrie
16 Cultural values
17 Mouth, slangily
18 Pastry finisher
19 Piece of the action
20 Peace offering #1: "___"
23 Normand of the silents
24 Mini-dog
25 Grounded speedsters
27 Hayworth husband ___ Khan
28 Satisfied sounds
31 Fly catcher
33 Sister
34 Plant firmly
36 Last Olds ever made
38 Peace offering #2: "___"
42 Plumber's gadget
43 Ill-tempered
44 Haifa's land: Abbr.
45 Heed the coxswain
48 Bleat
49 Great Society initiator's inits.
52 Toupees, slangily
54 "Hogwash!"
56 Cathedral topper
58 Peace offering #3: "___"
62 Laces into
63 Have the nerve
64 Trident-shaped letters
65 "Who's there?" reply
66 Blue-pencil
67 Alternative digest magazine
68 Flows slowly
69 Wall Street inits.
70 The "P" of PX

DOWN
1 Inhaler target
2 "Can you believe it?!"
3 Just around the corner
4 Home on the range
5 Can of worms, maybe
6 St. Louis landmark
7 Winter hazard
8 Blue feeling
9 Polite reply from a ranch hand
10 Dumas swordsman
11 "How's tricks?"
12 Like some soda bottles
13 157.5° from N
21 Hoosegow
22 Needle feature
26 ___-cone
29 SHO alternative
30 Do some quilting
32 Ship stabilizer
34 Caribou kin
35 Sot's symptoms, for short
37 ___ of the land
38 Wrap in fiberglass
39 Generous gifts
40 Center of activity
41 Division of history
42 Round Table title
46 Web address ending
47 Like some dummies
49 Deceives
50 Gray matter
51 Trendy travelers
53 Snail mail attachment
55 Apple-polisher
57 Toaster type
59 Fr. holy women
60 "Trinity" author
61 Where to put un chapeau
62 Towel stitching

by Harriet Clifton

ACROSS

1 Ump's call
5 Like some committees
10 White-bearded type
14 Rectangular cereal
15 Papal topper
16 Run perfectly
17 Eastern nurse
18 Overthrow, say
19 Prelude to a solution
20 Marinated dish
22 Gainsays
24 Eleanor's follower as first lady
25 Sing-along, of sorts
26 Group in power
29 Alpaca's relative
30 Banded stone
31 "Yikes!"
32 TV's Arthur
35 20-, 25-, 45- and 50-Across, in a way
39 Suffix with cannon
40 Bowling green, e.g.
41 "Maria ___" (1940's hit)
42 They form bonds
44 Unjust accusation
45 Flower-arranging art
48 Shia, e.g.
49 Some back-and-forth, briefly
50 Variety of pinball
54 Stadium section
55 Baker of song
57 ___ Cooper (popular car)
58 Flock members
59 Clan symbol

60 Compound with a hydroxyl group
61 It's typically thrown eight feet
62 Dodge
63 Like a Playboy Playmate

DOWN

1 "Scram!"
2 Sighed words
3 Cold feet, so to speak
4 Prime bit of trial evidence
5 Drill directive
6 Daggers
7 Mata ___ (spy)
8 ___ y Plata (Montana's motto)
9 Spice in Indian cuisine

10 ___ column
11 Part of a TV transmission
12 Rosetta Stone language
13 Demagnetize, maybe
21 Aden's land
23 Palindromic preposition
25 "Funny Girl" director Garson ___
26 Big Indian
27 "Omigosh!"
28 Be slack-jawed
29 Tobacco units
31 2003 Afghani film that won a Golden Globe for Best Foreign Language Film
32 Uncle Remus title

33 European erupter
34 P.D.Q.
36 Stretch out
37 Source of some brandy
38 Yesteryear
42 Best qualified
43 Eastern "way"
44 Turned into
45 Putzed around
46 Plains Indian
47 All fired up
48 Too full
50 Gyro holder
51 Shortest iron, in golf
52 James ___ Polk
53 Like olives or peanuts
56 Natl. Adoption Mo.

by Anne Garellick

26

ACROSS
1 Studied
10 Early course
15 Shared smoke
16 Blather
17 Judges
18 One year record
19 Proctor's instruction
20 It's in poetry
21 Family girl
22 Kind of ribs
24 Weighed down
26 Solid-colored pool ball
29 Cable channel
31 Music category
32 Exuded class
35 Eager player's cry
40 Having nobody owing anybody
41 Financial institution
43 Some twist it before eating
44 The world, according to Pistol, in "The Merry Wives of Windsor"
47 Slash
50 Overnight site
52 Monopoly deed
53 __-mo
54 Blue-blooded
59 Whelp
61 Dark
62 Thug's piece
64 Big dipper
68 In New Zealand, it means "normal"
69 Shift in steps
71 Retired
72 Indirect references
73 John on a farm
74 Purse taker

DOWN
1 Dress __ (resemble)
2 Fit (in)
3 Rover's owner
4 Sharp
5 Treaty topic
6 DHL competitor
7 Successful comic
8 "__ Love" (1957 #1 hit)
9 Reduced
10 One way to fly
11 Dan's buddy on "Roseanne"
12 Kind of closet
13 Quickly
14 Took out
23 Lecture follow-up
25 Texas school
26 "The Cosby Show" boy
27 Rolling
28 Confucius's "Book of __"
30 German dessert
33 Army member
34 Corporate department
36 Unduly
37 Portico adornments
38 Material
39 Beginning of a plea
42 Women's __
45 Shallow period
46 Soldier's reward
48 Food giant
49 Mishmash
51 One desiring change
54 One of the three H's
55 Stupid
56 Classroom fixture
57 Personnel director
58 Alfalfa's beloved
60 Summer party locale
63 Locker room supply
65 Christian name
66 Chaney and others
67 Start of Massachusetts' motto
70 Expected

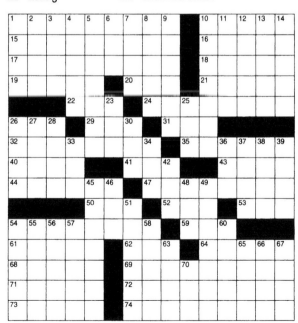

by Patrick Merrell

ACROSS

1 Airshow staple
12 Skip preceder
15 Catwoman, e.g.
16 "O the cannons ___ their rosy-flashing muzzles!": Whitman
17 Result of a big impact
19 Some accounting entries: Abbr.
20 Brand name on a white bottle
21 "When We Dead Awaken" dramatist
24 Hi-___
27 China's Zhou ___
28 "Children of the Tenements" author
29 Peggy Ashcroft and others
31 Numerical prefix
32 Negatively
33 Double-check, say
35 1970's radical grp.
36 Provider of partial coverage?
37 Certain polit. party
38 Pope's title
40 Concert ending
41 Quince, for one
42 Mine openings
43 Constitution: Abbr.
44 Kind of personality
46 Abbr. in many French street names
47 Pinups, perhaps
48 Foot bone
50 Winter Olympics powerhouse: Abbr.
51 "There's no way"
58 A third of nove
59 Old Colony's neighbor
60 Done, to Donne
61 Spy wear

DOWN

1 Flight
2 With 4-Down, some swimsuits
3 Giant of note
4 See 2-Down
5 Sticker
6 His mate
7 Verdi's "___ tu"
8 Raft
9 Goose, to Grégoire
10 Whenever
11 Political adviser Richard
12 It offers bedding and betting
13 Working
14 Some longhairs
18 Defensive comeback
21 Part of an underground spring crop
22 Forbes 400 listee
23 Novel subtitled "The Weaver of Raveloe"
24 Bartender dupers
25 "Seriously!"
26 Place out of sight
29 Friend of Froggy
30 Pseudonymous doctor
33 "From ___ to Mozart" (1980 documentary)
34 Some N.F.L.ers
39 Holdup
43 Aces
45 Spread like wildfire
47 Gloria Steinem's "___ Playboy Bunny"
49 Broad-topped hill, in the Southwest
50 Rock producer Talmy
52 "As It Happens" airer
53 End of peace?
54 Where Santa Fé is: Abbr.
55 Dance bit
56 It includes juillet
57 Super ___ (GameCube predecessor)

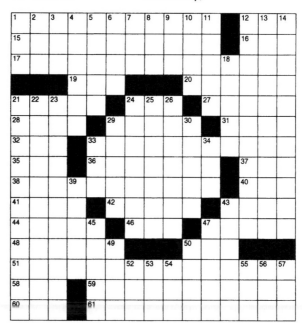

by Levi Denham

28

ACROSS

1 They go on and on
8 Microscopic animal that swims with whirling cilia
15 Francis ___, 17th-century English poet who wrote "A Feast for Worms"
16 Slippery
17 Cheerleading event
18 Kind of acid that dissolves gold
19 Whom People magazine once named the world's "sexiest classical musician"
20 Actress Martin who starred in TV's "National Velvet"
21 Author LeShan
22 Educational foundation?
25 Slowly entering
26 May in "Spider-Man," for one
27 Bellini title roles
28 ___ pie
29 No shrimp
32 How some old things go
33 Make ___ of
34 Didn't shuffle
37 Hollows
38 Copal and others
42 Summer camp fun on a lake
44 Literary pastiche
45 Came down from one's high horse?
46 Looking for big bucks?

47 Secure against jostling
49 City where Trotsky was exiled
50 "Jesus Christ Superstar" lyricist
51 Big goof
52 Cans under a dish
53 Workshop gizmos

DOWN

1 Stylish, square-jawed male model
2 Charioteer who precedes Apollo
3 Agree
4 University town with ZIP code 57006
5 Containing element #13
6 Blow up
7 Barbecue sound
8 Time-sharing locales
9 Exceed
10 Connie's portrayer, in "The Godfather"
11 British verb ending
12 Tweak
13 Show
14 Took it all back
20 River whose headwaters are near Lake Baikal
23 Bubbleheaded
24 Threatens violence
28 Jungian topic
29 Histories to overcome

30 "That was no joke"
31 Nice cop
32 It's a wrap
34 Women abducted by Romulus and his men
35 Roll (out)
36 Fig. in milligrams
38 Spiral: Prefix
39 Cooling-off period
40 Less blowzy
41 Red giants with zirconium oxide in their spectra
43 Inexpensive fur
48 Music sheet abbr.
49 Window boxes, for short?

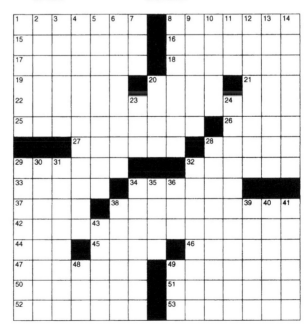

by Byron Walden

ACROSS

1 Top stories of barns
6 With 26-Across, Massachusetts resort area
10 Toot one's horn
14 Onetime Dutch fad item
15 "'Potpourri' for a thousand, ___"
16 Mother of Apollo and Artemis
17 Theater school study
18 ___ Ness monster
19 Natural soother
20 Any of the Stones or the Who, e.g.
23 Multichanneled
25 It may have screwdrivers on it
26 See 6-Across
27 Moving jerkily
31 English cathedral site
32 Bettor's promises, e.g.
34 Cave
36 White-collar crime investigators follow them
40 Patronize, as a restaurant
41 Barbie or Ken
44 Cumberland ___
47 Default modes
50 Vote in favor
51 Start of a cry by Juliet
53 Didn't talk smoothly
55 Sidestroke features
59 Hourglass fill
60 See 2-Down
61 Loathes
64 Look ___ (study)
65 Author Wiesel

66 Les ___-Unis
67 Shells out
68 Indoor arena feature
69 Not saying much

DOWN

1 Inc., abroad
2 With 60-Across, Thornton Wilder play
3 Recurred, as an ailment
4 East ___ (U.N. member since 2002)
5 They may be wide open
6 Tranquility
7 Outfielder Moises
8 Chest muscles, briefly

9 Most damning evidence, maybe
10 "The ___ Witch Project"
11 Tell
12 Lacking a key, in music
13 Is called
21 Keystone ___ (old comedy figure)
22 Spiny plants
23 Physics, for one: Abbr.
24 Overly
28 What "I" and "am" do
29 Niñas: Abbr.
30 Rich dessert
33 Unhappy
35 The "O" in G.O.P.
37 Church organ features
38 Deep-seated

39 Susan Lucci, notably
42 Strong alkaline
43 Batted first, with "off"
44 Grapevine contents
45 Obscure matters
46 Like the tops of dunce caps
48 Prefix with state
49 Fragrant pouch
52 Windows predecessor
54 Play ice hockey
56 Caramel candy brand
57 Sink's alternative
58 Elbow's lower counterpart
62 Aliens, for short
63 Reverse of NNW

by Ethan Cooper

ACROSS

1 Big maker of metal products
6 "The Fox and the Grapes" author
11 The "it" in "Step on it!"
14 Imam's declaration
15 Shelley's "Cheers" role
16 Prov. on Niagara Falls
17 Egg-shaped
18 E
20 London's Big ___
21 "Do the Right Thing" pizzeria
23 Actor Bruce
24 Good-for-nothing
26 Some Baltic residents
29 Jazz's Fitzgerald
30 Equals
33 Rodeo rope
34 "Must be something ___"
35 M
42 Massage deeply
43 Hotmail alternative
44 C
50 Classmate
51 Challenged
52 Get an ___ (ace)
53 Prenatal test, for short
55 Halloween wear
57 Morse Tony-winning role
59 Squared
62 Like a game in which batters bat .000
64 6 on a phone
65 Many an ex-dictator
66 Not just fat
67 Elton John, e.g.

68 Flip out
69 Michelins or Pirellis

DOWN

1 "This is ___ for Superman!"
2 Worms or grubs
3 Setting of the movie "Eight Crazy Nights"
4 Stable bit?
5 Drinks stirred in pitchers
6 Title subject of a 1975 Truffaut film
7 $E = mc^2$ (first presented 9/27/1905)
8 Mediterranean isl.
9 Yoko ___
10 One of the Ivys
11 Modern means of search

12 "Measure for Measure" villain
13 Minnesota college
19 Place
22 PC key
25 "Get ___ the Church on Time"
27 30-second spot, e.g.
28 Exam with a perfect score of 2400
30 Part of a chorus line?
31 Lizard: Prefix
32 Actress Lotte
36 Auctioneer's shout
37 Italian sports car, briefly
38 ___ avis
39 "Nuts!"
40 Event on the horizon

41 Ages and ages
44 Jerks
45 Sana'a native
46 Yoda, to Luke Skywalker
47 Elton John, e.g.
48 Collected
49 Nonvinyl records, briefly
54 Designer Cassini
56 Granny ___
58 Salt Lake City collegians
60 Prefix with skeleton
61 Darken
63 Formal Japanese wear

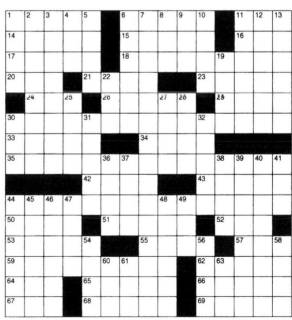

by Kevan Choset

ACROSS

1 Place to get sober
6 Prekindergartners
10 Repulsive one
14 Walled city in Spain
15 Uprising
16 Within: Prefix
17 Pirate's pal
18 Start to freeze?
19 Nautilus skipper
20 Committee head's timepiece?
23 A.C. measure
26 Prior to, to Prior
27 Ones running through California
28 Trojan hero
30 Tuckered out
32 Ice-cream request?
34 Part of T.G.I.F.: Abbr.
37 Barbra's "A Star Is Born" co-star
38 One way to the www
39 North African port
40 Former J.F.K. lander
41 Spice wagon?
45 Lisa of "The Cosby Show"
46 Gilda of "S.N.L."
47 Phoebe orbits it
50 Champion's award
51 Explosive inits.
52 Gibberish from zoo animals?
56 Where a power play may occur
57 Orbital period
58 Radium discoverer
62 Start of a crystal gazer's statement
63 Library catalog abbr.
64 Passes over
65 Saucy
66 Turn down
67 Dummies

DOWN

1 Rear-end, e.g.
2 Stowe heroine
3 Bomb's opposite
4 A Baldwin
5 Seasoning from the laurel tree
6 Try to locate
7 Sty cry
8 Oz visitor
9 Get starched?
10 Opposite of "At ease!"
11 Actor Patrick
12 Fess up to
13 Some are sliding
21 Guesstimate phrase
22 Porch chair material
23 Pigskin carriers
24 Crocodile __
25 Dark
29 Loop transports
30 Patton player
31 Game you can't play left-handed
33 Like a white Bengal tiger
34 Battle line
35 "Nevermore" speaker
36 Like neon
39 Moth-eaten
41 Stopper
42 Ticked off
43 60's dance
44 Where Yarmouth is
45 Bailer's need
47 Temporary money
48 Wake up
49 Copier need
50 Singer Simon
53 Big do
54 James of "Thief"
55 Ring contest
59 Free (of)
60 "Am __ believe . . . ?"
61 Part of a slot-car track

by Randall J. Hartman

ACROSS

1 ___ cherry
5 Zoot suit feature
10 "Pardon"
14 Spray target, perhaps
15 Spanish for "poplar"
16 ___ avis
17 With 25-, 45- and 58-Across, some advice by 36-Across
20 Nets with floats
21 Emir's land
22 Sixth-century year
24 Singer Coolidge
25 See 17-Across
32 Pizarro's conquest
33 Something bad to be caught in
34 August
35 A cat, but rarely a rat
36 See 17-Across
38 Prefix with puncture
39 1974 top 10 hit with Spanish lyrics
42 Necessity for some, in order to go to the movies
45 See 17-Across
49 Enraptured
50 Elia Kazan's autobiography
53 Fraternity character
54 Supplement
58 See 17-Across
61 "Far out, man!"
62 Sole saver
63 Nod's significance
64 Steaming
65 "Ain't ___ Sweet?"
66 Card game with forfeits

DOWN

1 They may hang by the neck
2 Shelved
3 "___ get it!"
4 One of the Munsters
5 Tommy Rettig's costar in 1950's TV
6 H.S. subject
7 Kung ___ chicken
8 Ambulance staffer, for short
9 Take a peek
10 Decorative pottery and such
11 "Aren't we the comedian?!"
12 ". . . ___ saw Elba"
13 K follower
18 Blasts out
19 On the perimeter
23 Ferry destination, possibly
24 One who's sorry
25 Appurtenance for Santa
26 Month "The Motorcycle Diaries" begins
27 Four pairs
28 Balsam
29 Playing marble
30 Half of a 1980's TV team
31 Drag through the mud
36 Small knot
37 Where ships go
40 Mine passages
41 Verizon, for one
43 "Quite possibly"
44 Lead character in a Mario Puzo novel
46 Loosened (up)
47 "___ hollers, let . . ."
48 Hardly go-getters
50 On the road
51 E. S. ___, old game company famous for Yahtzee and Bingo
52 Chemical suffixes
55 Twofold
56 Wynken, Blynken and Nod, e.g.
57 Capital NW of Drammen
59 Medical suffix
60 "That feels good!"

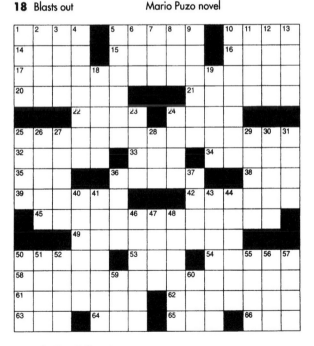

by Sam Bellotto Jr.

33

ACROSS

1 Risky person to neck with
8 Place for an embedded journalist
15 Entices
16 The Angelic Doctor
17 Shamed
18 Manuscript headings
19 Like some dresses and drinks
20 ___ dare
21 Pith
22 New N.F.L. team of 1950
24 Scale composition
25 Prefix with cab
28 Salmon ___
29 Script writer
30 Pinwheel turner
33 Shogun's capital
36 Reputation ruiner
38 Friend's possessive
39 Lack of starch
40 Dram
41 Eastern way
42 Attraction at Chicago's Field Museum
43 Advice for the easily distracted
46 Like some excuses
48 It's known for its bell ringers
49 Common bar order, briefly
50 More supernatural
54 Like veal calves
56 Roald Dahl title character
57 Broke in, e.g.
58 Parrotlike behavior

59 Seer's "revelation"
60 Considering that

DOWN

1 Cheerless
2 Cover-up
3 "C'mon, be ___"
4 "That's fine," in France
5 Work with a flashlight
6 Be quiescent
7 "Do go on . . ."
8 Tips off
9 Liquid, to a pharmacist
10 Polish
11 Matura diamond, actually
12 Source of some tears
13 Certain shell liner

14 Leaders of San Salvador
20 Like many ice-skating spins
23 "Orlando" novelist
24 Land
25 Head-turner
26 Impress clearly
27 Heavy hauler
29 Town south of San Luis Obispo
31 Parting word
32 Emanations, old-style
33 Kaffiyehed commander
34 Spoil, with "on"
35 African grazer
37 Beyond what is openly said
40 Outing
43 Big-name

44 Like Little Bo-Peep's charges
45 Would-be studs
46 Stuffy sort, in slang
47 River in Hades
49 Lived
51 "Would ___?"
52 Best seen on-screen
53 No fancy threads
55 It may be casual: Abbr.
56 Small gull

by Nancy Kavanaugh

34

ACROSS
1 Sting, basically
5 Vera Miles, in 1948
15 City surrounded on two sides by Toiyabe National Forest
16 "Is this really my fault?"
17 About
18 House style
19 Video store section
21 It opens Letterman's "Viewer Mail"
22 Berkshire, e.g.
23 It might get busted
25 Wrestler Flair, 10-time N.W.A. world heavyweight champion
26 Straight up
28 Jake's lover in "The Sun Also Rises"
30 Hearty meat dish
31 Bunch of sitcom characters
32 Fellahs
33 Stretched out
34 Calf muscle
37 Upset
41 Online greeting
42 Pontiff for just 26 days in 1605
43 Choice for un votant
44 ___ track
45 Drink that's stirred
46 Bird of the American Arctic that migrates south
49 Forger

51 Mistaken
53 Hard ___
54 Zip
55 More than a little off
56 Scooby-Doo and others
57 1979 revolution locale

DOWN
1 "Masterpiece Theatre" it ain't
2 Change from a hit to an error, say
3 West Indies island
4 Disappearing word
5 Humanities degs.
6 Entreats
7 Start to write?
8 Laugh maker
9 Actor Yaphet ___, of TV's "Homicide"
10 Equipped
11 What an A is not
12 Took pleasure in
13 Shower cap at a motel, maybe
14 Culls
20 1930's–50's Arab ruler
24 Univ. military programs
27 Hunter with a middle initial of J
28 Shows disdain
29 Indian dignitary
31 John Deere product
33 Los Angeles suburb
34 Picking up
35 Reagan Supreme Court nominee
36 1961 Michelangelo Antonioni film a k a "The Night"
37 Seasonal recurrence
38 Watch
39 Carnival displays
40 "You said it!"
42 Home of the Chiefs in minor-league baseball
44 Hooked up and left
47 "Now that's awesome!"
48 Chap
50 Landlocked land of 12 million
52 Bunch of fun

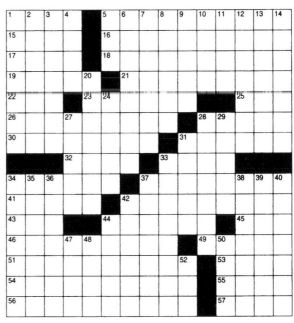

by Joe DiPietro

ACROSS

1 Top
5 ___ Lingus
8 Sleeping sickness transmitter
14 Film ___ (movie genre)
15 Multiplatinum album with the 2002 hit "Ain't It Funny"
16 Met productions
17 Star of 64-Across
19 Dancer Ginger
20 2004 World Series "curse" beaters
21 Exchange blows
23 Summer drink
24 Henry Ford's son
25 Number of 17-Across in 64-Across
27 Putdown
29 Shakespeare's "___ Like It"
30 Explosive
33 "___, meeny, miney, mo"
35 Sand
38 Catchphrase of 25-Across
43 Out of kilter
44 "___ Lisa"
45 Bread with seeds
46 Paint palette accompanier
50 Artist Bonheur
52 Gadget for 25-Across
55 Check for odors
59 ___ Mahal
60 Part of an interstate
61 Quite the party
62 Small garage capacity
64 Campy 1960's hit sitcom
66 Spin

67 "Xanadu" band, for short
68 "Don't look ___!"
69 Fellow
70 Ex-G.I.'s grp.
71 Gifts at Honolulu International Airport

DOWN

1 Tennis's Agassi
2 Murmured
3 Watches, as a store
4 Wipes clean
5 Comet competitor
6 Nightmarish street, in film
7 Martini & ___ vermouth
8 Hebrew scrolls
9 Like Corvettes and Mustangs
10 Brain scan, for short
11 Money manager
12 Famed New York restaurateur
13 Elizabethan earl
18 Dressed (up)
22 Links org.
25 Rubik who invented Rubik's Cube
26 Bear or Berra
28 180° turn, slangily
30 Bygone carrier
31 "This instant!"
32 Some airplanes
34 "Tasty!"
36 Old-fashioned Christmas trim
37 Summer shirt
39 Ancient Greek instrument
40 Yawn inducer
41 British musician Brian
42 Ropes in
47 Still awake at 1 a.m., say
48 Generous one
49 Darlin'
51 20 Questions category
52 Tempest
53 Vietnam's capital
54 Israeli desert
56 Angered
57 Physicist Enrico
58 Honors in style
61 Pack away
63 Cool dude, in jazz
65 Keebler baker, supposedly

by Roy Leban

ACROSS

1 Mongrel dogs
5 Color of honey
10 On the road
14 Meltable food item
15 One of the Flintstones
16 Salad cheese
17 Keyboard key
19 Go smoothly
20 No Mr. Nice Guy
21 Joint with a cap
22 View in northern Italy
23 Cantankerous
25 Throw off track
27 Dates
29 16-Across is preserved in it
32 "Surely you ___!"
35 Geronimo, e.g.
39 Powder holder
40 Que. neighbor
41 Theme of this puzzle
42 Fraction of a joule
43 The year 56
44 Toughen, as glass
45 O.T.B. postings
46 First president to marry while in office
48 Dovetail
50 Memory gaps
54 "Enough!"
58 Clubmates
60 "Quickly!"
62 Imam's faith
63 Door sign
64 Where thunderstorms may occur
66 Teeming
67 Iraq's ___ Triangle
68 Mary Kay rival
69 Manipulative one
70 Bakery supply
71 Make (one's way)

DOWN

1 Hearst magazine, familiarly
2 Gastric woe
3 Played over
4 Most quickly
5 Saddler's tool
6 Do some work on a dairy farm
7 Strawberry ___
8 Toaster, or roaster
9 Autumn toiler
10 Fling
11 Popular
12 On
13 Swerves at sea
18 Cousin of a harp
24 Long (for)
26 Genesis son
28 Board game turn
30 Encyclopedia reader from A to Z, say
31 Caviar, essentially
32 Bump hard
33 It's a sin
34 Painting of flowers, e.g.
36 Barbary beast
37 Secretive sort
38 Lady of Troy
41 Stadium rollout
45 Electrical principle
47 Parade day
49 Make dirty
51 Fresh-mouthed
52 Suffix with Roman
53 Spot for sweaters
55 Oil source
56 Wouldn't stop
57 Touch up
58 Lima's land
59 W.W. II enemy
61 Gives zero stars to
65 Torched

by Barry C. Silk

ACROSS

1 Derby features
6 James who wrote "The Postman Always Rings Twice"
10 Golden Fleece transporter
14 State-named avenues in Washington, essentially
15 Plot part
16 Zig or zag
17 First-stringers
18 Obits, basically
19 A penny is a small one
20 Start of a quizzical Bob Seger lyric
23 "___ chance!"
24 Employed pols
25 Pin holders
27 Hams it up for the camera
29 With 46-Across, song containing the lyric in this puzzle
31 Dowdy one
34 Venomous snake
35 Mark of mediocrity
36 Spy novelist Deighton
37 Lyric, part 2
41 H, to Homer
42 Interject
43 "Scream" director Craven
44 Performed satisfactorily
46 See 29-Across
49 Buttinsky, e.g.
51 Wrap brand
52 Submit to gravity
53 Bawls
57 End of the lyric

61 Race pace
62 Watched warily
63 Good and steamed
64 Clinton's attorney general
65 Stage solo
66 Lorelei, notably
67 Mideast port
68 Plenty
69 Passed out

DOWN

1 Muscles
2 Pi, for one
3 Latin clarifier
4 Soccer superstar
5 California's ___ Valley
6 Cruise ship accommodations
7 Tums' targets

8 Monopoly token
9 Site for brooding
10 Sporty Studebaker
11 Gave up
12 Figure out
13 Load from a lode
21 Go after 13-Down
22 Mauna ___ Observatory
26 Fajita filler
28 "America's Next Top Model" airer
29 Shade of blond
30 Student no.
31 Heels alternative
32 Like Lucille Ball
33 Too pink, say
34 Sympathetic sounds

38 Fess (up)
39 Made one
40 Passing thoughts, for short?
45 "I swear!"
47 Be a servant to
48 Neither Rep. nor Dem.
49 Bamboo lovers
50 Teamwork spoiler
52 Yarn unit
54 "Butterfield 8" author
55 Some kind of nut
56 Hägar's dog, in the funnies
58 Shipshape
59 Newbie
60 Feral
61 ___-la-la

by Nancy Salomon

38

ACROSS

1 Pepperdine University site
7 "___ little spice to your life"
11 Rotund
14 1950 Asimov classic
15 You name it
16 Blood-type letters
17 Each animal has one in "Old MacDonald Had a Farm"
18 Crux
19 Excessively
20 Shakespearean bird call
23 Devils and Angels, e.g.
27 Highest score in baccarat
28 Many an office has one
29 Forearm part
30 Learns
32 "Laughed myself silly!"
34 National Poetry Month
38 Set of advantages
39 National airline of Afghanistan
40 Request on a memo from the boss
41 Advice of patience
44 Like some chest pain
46 X ___ xylophone
47 Engrave
50 Ones making pantry raids?
51 They usually have two runners on
52 Radar's hometown, in "M*A*S*H"
55 Kind of tax
56 Been in bed
57 Officially choose
62 Epilogue
63 Prong
64 Item literally useful in reading the answers to 20-, 32-, 41- and 52-Across
65 Late July birth
66 Linear
67 Nutso

DOWN

1 Start to take?
2 ___ nouveau
3 Mauna ___
4 ___ Saud, founder of Saudi Arabia
5 Yahoos
6 Jazz venue
7 Worry
8 "Stop procrastinating!"
9 Close pitch
10 No pro
11 Islamic declaration
12 "It's ___ time!"
13 Kind of fairy
21 N.Y. Liberty's org.
22 Ward site
23 Ballet apparel
24 Sneak off
25 Win by ___
26 Dolphinfish
30 Grazed
31 Italian port
33 Yemeni port
35 Bring up
36 Grants-___
37 Many yards
39 Azores locale: Abbr.
41 Bolivian underground?
42 Off-key
43 Kiln
45 "Sir ___ and the Green Knight"
47 Oil holder
48 Rope
49 Unit in a multiunit building
51 Seattle athlete, briefly
53 Low woman
54 Scot's tops
58 Legendary stick figure
59 Eng. neighbor
60 Feminist org. since 1966
61 "___ me!"

by Daniel C. Bryant

39

ACROSS

1 Refuse transportation?
5 Dust remover
15 One of a skeletal pair
16 Must
17 Spin
18 Uffizi collection
19 Engineering ring
21 Falling out
22 Derisive interjection
23 Put down
25 Hereditary ruler?
27 Inquisition target
29 Parlor pieces
33 Takes the wrong way?
34 "___ do you good"
36 Pillow padding
37 March word
38 Fraudulent acts
40 Greek letter spelled out at the start of a Beatles title?
41 Val d'___, France, 1992 Olympics skiing site
43 Astronomical effect
44 Faux pas
45 Propels, in a way
47 Insulting one
49 Way in or out
51 Folds
53 Swear words?
56 Air-freight, e.g.
58 Where Jehu ruled
59 Citrus-y drink
62 Oompah-paher
63 Emptied
64 Subj. with graphs
65 Alarmist
66 Chapter 11 issue

DOWN

1 Coastal resident's hurricane worry
2 Completely replace the staff
3 Danced the milonga
4 Ones refusing transportation?
5 Formal requirement
6 Sou'wester, e.g.
7 Swedish monopolist Kreuger
8 Vincent's successor as baseball commissioner
9 Cut in a fight, maybe
10 Nonconformists
11 Nickelodeon Chihuahua
12 Jazz singer Anita
13 Not esa or esta
14 Armyworm, eventually
20 "Maid of Athens, ___ We Part" (Byron poem)
24 Make an emergency landing
26 Spacewalk, for NASA
28 Traction enhancer
30 Bunk
31 Emphatic negative
32 LP problem
33 Antique damage
35 Amethyst shade
38 Misleading
39 Like resorts, typically
42 Awesome
44 Under way
46 Lug
48 Old Mario Bros. console
50 It's wavy in São Paulo
52 Partial approach?
53 Target for nails
54 Charity
55 Something wordless to read
57 Short-lived particle
60 Preserve
61 Parochial schoolteacher

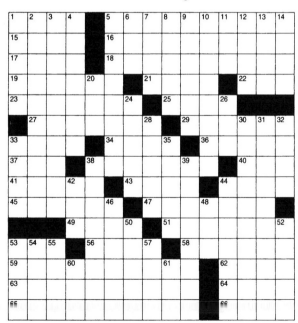

by Manny Nosowsky

ACROSS

1 Some clowning around
11 Ancient Briton
15 Hotel amenity
16 Get __ deal
17 Creep
18 Oil spot
19 Smarts
20 It may be given with a bow
22 Yellows or grays
23 Something hard to get nowadays by phone
24 1935 movie starring Helen Gahagan as Queen Hash-a-Mo-Tep of Kor
25 Jeweler's gadget
26 Bisque fleck
27 Appellate judge, often
28 Certain craft hobbyist
29 Circulated some winter airs
32 Kind of block
33 Equus hemionus
34 Places that serve O.J. beside the links?
35 "__ Out," 2003 Tony winner for Best Choreography
36 Fret over, slangily
37 10-4
40 Not a walk in the park
42 Closing bars
43 " 'Deed I Do" singer
44 Lost all patience
45 __ row
46 "May I interrupt you?"

48 Item component usually seen in threes or fours
49 "We're not getting back together"
50 Some hosp. records
51 Area of limited growth

DOWN

1 98 and 99, typically
2 "Knock it off!"
3 She played Musette to Gish's Mimi in "La Boheme," 1926
4 Things that are out of bounds
5 They knock back lots
6 Prefix with syllabic
7 Valued
8 "Ain't gonna happen"
9 Let
10 Time out?
11 Small favors that go to your head
12 Old TV drama set in San Francisco
13 Shroud of Torino?
14 Some middle-schoolers
21 Slip on a new piece of clothing?
23 Engine unit
25 Hourlong introduction?
27 Works the old bean

28 Like a liberal arts education
29 Consummate
30 Taking in too little
31 Wanting it all
32 Groggy query
34 "Gimme"
36 __ Sunday a k a Quinquagesima
37 Jiver's greeting
38 Post operative?
39 Unmistakable
41 They're light-seeking
42 Staffs
44 Queen's domain
47 Up-to-date, informally

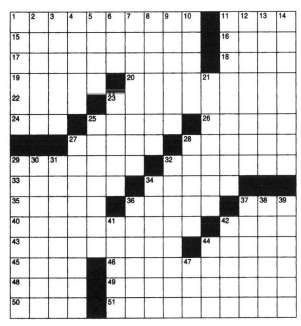

by Byron Walden

ACROSS

1 Swimming units
5 Not tight
10 Possess
14 Geometry calculation
15 City on the Missouri
16 Asia's __ Sea
17 Laurel or Musial
18 VCR button
19 Pastrami purveyor
20 Actor Quaid transgressed
23 Giant Hall-of-Famer
26 Not as much
27 Condoleezza Rice's department
28 Bongos
30 Two-striper in the Army: Abbr.
32 Draft org.
33 Frontiersman Boone did some carpentry
38 Bridge
39 St. Nick
40 Capital on a fjord
44 Actor Hickman showed boredom
47 Fuel economy stat.
50 Non-earthlings, for short
51 Asinine
52 Move on all fours
54 Hydrofluoric __
57 Exxon product
58 President Ford stared fiercely
62 As a czar, he was terrible
63 Home of the University of Maine
64 __ Romeo (sports car)
68 Olympic sled
69 Assign to, as blame
70 Potting material
71 Popular jeans
72 Fencing weapons
73 Very large

DOWN

1 __ Cruces, N.M.
2 "But is it __?"
3 Vegetable that rolls
4 Hourglass contents
5 Greene of "Bonanza"
6 Black cats, to the superstitious
7 Caravan's stop
8 "__ a Lady" (Tom Jones hit)
9 Diner sign
10 Lacked, briefly
11 Sporting venues
12 Gentlemen's gentlemen
13 Omits, in pronunciation
21 Ultimatum ender
22 Man or Wight
23 __ and ends
24 Links hazard
25 Albacore or yellowfin
29 Intellect
30 Hit with a ticket
31 Thespian production
34 Future D.A.'s exam
35 Ayes' opposite
36 Cape __, Mass.
37 Low in spirits
41 Hose problem
42 __ the Hyena
43 Praiseful poems
45 Place to make a wish
46 Assistant
47 Montreal university
48 Advance look, informally
49 It may have a remote-activated door
53 Declines
54 "Home __," Macaulay Culkin movie
55 Tippy craft
56 Numbered clubs
59 Latest news, slangily
60 Stagehand
61 Sprinter's event
65 Singer Rawls
66 Tiniest amount to care
67 "Cakes and __" (Maugham novel)

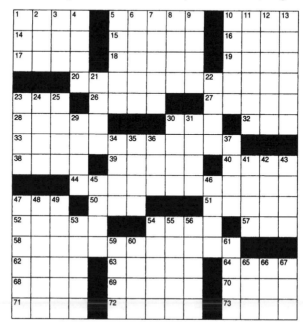

by Holden Baker

42

ACROSS

1 Mrs. Loopner player
7 Tells a bedtime story
14 Free drinks set-up
16 Mr. Blues player
17 Tickler of the ivories
18 Figured out, as secret writing
19 Show that debuted 10/11/1975, for short
20 Buffet table heater
22 Hail Mary, e.g.
23 King, in Cádiz
24 Bard's nightfall
25 Wearies
28 Syr. neighbor
29 Weekend Update anchor
34 Les États-___
35 Literary piece
36 Wretched
37 Longstanding 19-Across opener
40 Kuwaiti leaders: Var.
41 Take a swing
42 Old Venetian official
43 Announcer for 19-Across
44 Org. for Mariners
45 Lachesis and Clotho, in myth
46 Ground breaker
47 Ottoman ruler
48 University mil. group
52 Terrible trial
54 Network of 19-Across
57 Mistakenly
59 New York's ___ Bridge

61 Samurai tailor player
62 Medal giver
63 Naps, for señores
64 Ms. Conehead player

DOWN

1 Police
2 ___ arms
3 Genuine
4 Old cable TV inits.
5 Nile birds
6 Foul
7 Ms. Roseanne Roseannadanna player
8 Keep an ___ (watch)
9 Dog breeder's assn.
10 Withdraw from, as a case
11 Kind of water
12 Sailing ropes
13 Bookie's figure
15 Hwy.
21 Looked like
23 Tend to, as a barren lawn
25 Kentucky Derby drink
26 True inner self
27 Springboard performer
28 Phrase of commitment
29 Intimidate
30 The best of times
31 Under way
32 Power glitch
33 Actress Sommer and others
35 Surgeon's locales, quickly
36 Dripping
38 To and ___

39 Collar
44 Mr. Escuela player
45 Catlike
46 Big to-do
47 Von Richthofen's title
48 Barbecue fare
49 R.E.M.'s "The ___ Love"
50 Prefix with conference
51 Vineyards of high quality
53 Biblical suffix
54 Benchmark
55 La ___ Tar Pits
56 Foot ailment
58 String after Q
60 Close a show

by Mike Torch

ACROSS

1 Fudge maker?
5 Iowa's ___ Society
10 Asian nation suffix
14 A lot?
15 Like early PC graphics
16 Mall aid
17 Start of a quip
20 Big bird
21 Source of iron
22 Pound sound
23 Some are famous
27 Unearthly
30 Elvis trademark
31 Induce rain from
33 Claimer's cry
34 Grant-in-___
36 Milky Way and others
38 City, state, ___
39 Quip, part 2
43 "Yo!"
44 Times to revel, maybe
45 Not the handsomest dog
46 Surface figure
48 Ones who've gone splitsville
50 Circus Maximus attire
54 Vas deferens and others
56 Place for carved initials
58 Top guns
60 Circus Maximus greeting
61 MP3 player maker
62 End of the quip
67 ___ of the earth
68 "You've got mail" hearer
69 Lily family member

70 Four-time Indy winner
71 Rotten
72 Uncool sort

DOWN

1 Boutonnieres' places
2 One found just around the block?
3 Pique
4 Account overseer, for short
5 Car discontinued in 2004
6 Grounds crew
7 "Exodus" hero
8 Bring home
9 Pasty-faced
10 Like hair at salons
11 Gold medal, e.g.

12 Lunched
13 Opposite of paleo-
18 Like some women's jeans
19 ___ time (course slot)
24 Hotfoot it
25 Demeaning one
26 Use wax on
28 Egyptian sacred bird
29 Empath's skill
32 Coffeemaker style
35 Went off the deep end?
37 Sing "K-K-K-Katy," say
39 Big silver exporter
40 Nice things to look at
41 Counter call

42 1974 Marty Feldman comic-horror role
43 Took to the cleaners
47 For no profit
49 Ready for dinner
51 Fountain sound
52 Hold fast
53 Did toe loops, say
55 "Quiet!" locale
57 Part of the mnemonic for EGBDF
59 Started a triathlon
62 Hip-hop "cool"
63 Noted resident of the Dakota
64 Milne marsupial
65 Off one's feed
66 Actor McKellen

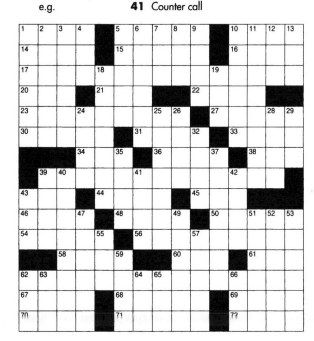

by Paul Guttormsson

44

ACROSS
1 One born near the Butt of Lewis
5 Dish eaten with a spork
9 Dark-skinned fruit
13 One-sixth of an inch
14 Lose power
15 Football Hall-of-Famer Ronnie
16 Helpful multiple-choice answer
19 "I think we should"
20 "Later"
21 Important licensing org.
22 Chums
23 Helpful multiple-choice answer
30 Much of suburbia
31 Bit of butter
32 Nomadic warrior of the Old West
33 Sugar suffix
34 Darn
35 Swiss Alp
37 Helpful multiple-choice answer
41 Life instinct, to Freud
42 Aves.
43 Echevarria who played Santa Ana in 2004's "The Alamo"
46 Prepare for a wild ride
50 Helpful multiple-choice answer . . . or is it?
52 "True!"
53 Inventor, of a sort
54 Cheers
55 Opening for peace talks
56 Trees used to make archery bows
57 Baseball's Eddie, 1952 All-Star for the Senators

DOWN
1 Fix, in a way
2 Formally honor
3 Newspaperman Arthur ___ Sulzberger
4 Car brake light holder, once
5 It's often flipped
6 Sweetheart
7 Arbor leader
8 Diver's duds
9 Least straightforward
10 Mentally sluggish
11 Roman emperor for just three months
12 Accusatory words
17 Divisions
18 Cold war enemy
22 Muscle
23 Like-minded individuals
24 Creator of the Tammany Hall tiger
25 The America's Cup trophy, e.g.
26 They're guarded at the Olympics
27 Boss of fashion
28 Calif.-Fla. route
29 Like the Sahara
34 Kind of pie
35 Seconds
36 Printing on some cigar wrappers
38 Chicken
39 Charlie's Angels, e.g.
40 Fragrant compounds
43 Computer menu option
44 Whiskey fermenter
45 Requester of "As Time Goes By"
46 Writer of "Saint Joan"
47 Word before field or shirt
48 Name on many prints
49 Diet of worms locale?
51 Draw

by Patrick Merrell

ACROSS

1 Historic trials
7 High-tech heart, for short
10 Somewhere over the rainbow
14 One affected by a strike
15 Like some devils?
17 Question upon hearing an accent
19 Host
20 Surface
21 Buck passer?
22 Particle stream
23 Possible penicillin target
25 Capital of Cambodia
28 It's not out of the ordinary
31 Put ___ (shove off)
33 Factor in some acad. probations
34 Starchy
36 Dramatic opening
38 Buck passer?
41 Kutcher who hosted TV's "Punk'd"
42 Horse-drawn vehicle
43 It may go for mi. and mi.
44 Sentencing request
46 A load
48 Point in the right direction?
50 Pageant put-on
52 Starter's aid
54 "Black" day in the stock market crash, 10/29/1929: Abbr.
56 "Don't be so shy!"
57 Ring sport

58 "Same thing, really"
62 Aged
63 Onetime Missouri natives
64 Corporeal canal
65 Sign of a crowd
66 With 9-Down, tops

DOWN

1 Not just bickering
2 Mehrabad International Airport site
3 Intelligence concern
4 Not at all lethargic
5 Windsor, for one
6 Comes (to)
7 Rally Sport, e.g.
8 Wage earners
9 See 66-Across
10 Concerning
11 Curriculum requirement, often
12 Te ___
13 Kind of sleep
16 Fizzle
18 Knocking noise
24 Topping for fish or meat
26 Thrusted thing
27 Nest
29 Etymologist's concern
30 Classic comedy film about gender-role reversal
32 Succeed in a big way
35 "Déjeuner sur l'herbe" artist

37 Nevada's second-largest county
38 Thun's river
39 Court org. since 1881
40 Wood problem
45 Comparatively creamy
47 Gordon ___ a k a Sting
49 Coach
51 It's negative
53 With 59-Down, unimpressive
55 Some aliens take it: Abbr.
57 Vulnerable gap
58 ___ Friday's
59 See 53-Down
60 Writing: Abbr.
61 East Lansing sch.

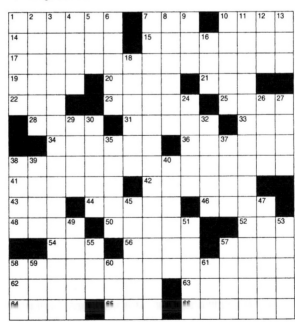

by Michael Shteyman

46

ACROSS

1 Like some Old Masters
8 Epithets
14 Flop
16 Complete circuit
17 Runner's place
18 "Casablanca" words repeated before "as if it were the last time"
19 Not hard
20 Flexible fastener
22 Pickled
23 11-member grp.
24 Public debt instrument
25 18-Across speaker
26 Top
28 Amalfi articles
29 Chemical ending
30 Better than O.K.
32 Cantina request
37 Wilde and Yeats
38 ___-jongg
39 Trudge
42 Range rover
43 Shelter dug into a hillside
44 Itty bits
46 Geezers' grunts
47 "___ of the Times" (1966 Petula Clark hit)
48 Automated answering machine base
50 Petulance
51 "Likewise"
52 "Out of the question"
54 Cut
55 Sleeper, for one
56 Builds
57 Arch sites

DOWN

1 Hustle
2 Port from which the Spanish Armada departed in 1588
3 Goth's look enhancer
4 Like a brig
5 Final, as a deal
6 Penn name
7 Info request from a computer dating service: Abbr.
8 Evildoer of Asgard
9 Dill relative
10 Cronies
11 Catcher for Whitey in the 1960's Yankees
12 Veneer
13 Floors it
15 Becomes competitive
21 Military practice
23 Name
26 Pinned attire
27 Skin refresher
30 Org. whose first president general was first lady Caroline Harrison
31 Suffix with ball
33 Walloping
34 Atmosphere
35 Fund designation
36 Dilutants
39 Float like a butterfly, say
40 Construction machine
41 Indolent
43 Not on the level
45 Utah senator who lent his name to a 1930 tariff act
47 Prey for a ladybug
49 Time immemorial
50 View by computer tomography
53 ". . . ___ quit!"

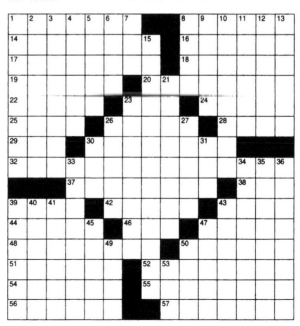

by Paula Gamache

ACROSS
1 Unravel, as a cord
5 Hand support
9 Fissures
14 Christmas season
15 To be, in Toulon
16 Messages via MSN.com, e.g.
17 "__ small world!"
18 Extended family
19 Backside
20 Old-fashioned
23 Nonverbal O.K.'s
24 Author Harper __
25 Amer. soldiers
28 Result of a hung jury, maybe
31 Fit __ fiddle
34 Fess up (to)
36 Driver's lic. and such
37 +
38 Fundamental
42 __ liquor
43 Two halves
44 "All in the Family" spinoff
45 The whole ball of wax
46 Mt. Rushmore material
49 "Law & Order" fig.
50 Shipwreck signal
51 Instrument hit with a hammer
53 Petty
59 Lethal snake
60 Yankee nickname starting 2004
61 Workbench attachment
63 "Doe, __, a female . . ."
64 Sagan or Sandburg

65 Glimpse
66 It might be 18 oz. on a cereal box
67 Safe sword
68 __ the wiser

DOWN
1 Memo letters
2 Justice __ Bader Ginsburg
3 By the same token
4 Long (for)
5 Ebb
6 "Finally!"
7 Tehran's land
8 What usurers do
9 Gas up again
10 Spitting __
11 Weapon of 59-Across
12 Wee
13 Underhanded

21 After a fashion, informally
22 Really good time
25 Alpha, beta, __ . . .
26 Perfect
27 Wee
29 Turn red, as a strawberry
30 Wedding vow
31 Not silently
32 Luxury leather
33 Liability's opposite
35 Cousin __ of "The Addams Family"
37 School fund-raising grp.
39 Like the Vikings
40 Genetic stuff
41 Change, as the Constitution

46 Fun park car
47 Tune out
48 Walk like a little 'un
50 It fits into a nut
52 First, as a name
53 Lymph bump
54 "Yeah, sure"
55 Open fabric
56 Amount not to care
57 Soybean paste
58 Armchair athlete's channel
59 Pop-top's place
62 Storm's center

by Gregory E. Paul

ACROSS

1 ___ Brockovich, Julia Roberts title role
5 Mex. misses
10 Tom, Dick or Harry
14 1998 N.L. M.V.P. from Chicago
15 Sports hiree
16 Sen. Bayh of Indiana
17 See 35-Across
20 Ladies of Lisbon
21 Crowbar, e.g.
22 "I've Got ___ in Kalamazoo"
23 Soccer ___
25 See 35-Across
30 Geniuses' group
31 12/24 or 12/31
32 Golfer Ballesteros
34 Samuel's teacher
35 This puzzle's theme, succinctly
39 Gen-___ (boomer's kid)
40 Shakespeare's stream
42 Hood's gun
43 Rhone tributary
45 See 35-Across
49 Cold war inits.
50 "___ No Mountain High Enough" (1970 #1 hit)
51 Underground Railroad user
54 Least drunk
58 See 35-Across
61 Follower of inter or et
62 "Marat/Sade" playwright
63 Statement to a judge
64 Chicken cordon ___
65 Cosmetician Lauder
66 Teamster's rig

DOWN

1 A.B.A. members' titles
2 Lecherous sort
3 "Beauty ___ the eye . . ."
4 Famous name in hot dogs
5 Japanese beetle, e.g.
6 Isle ___ National Park
7 Small amounts
8 90° from down: Abbr.
9 Any ship
10 Unbeatable foe
11 Tel ___, Israel
12 Luxuriant locks
13 M.I.T. grad., often
18 Bowser's identification
19 Diva Gluck
23 "Outta my way!"
24 Prime S.S.S. classification
25 Probe, with "into"
26 Bagel choice
27 Major mattress maker
28 Nettled
29 Each's companion
30 "___ culpa"
33 Bard's before
36 Soufflé needs
37 Asian goat
38 Holder of claimed property
41 ___ riche
44 Persian governors
46 Hand-me-down
47 Supposed founder of Taoism
48 Nucleic acid sugar
51 Strike defier
52 Vegetate
53 Gallic girlfriend
54 Fit of pique
55 Creator of Perry and Della
56 Goblet feature
57 Bangkok native
59 Have a tab
60 Jazz's Montgomery

by Jay Leatherman

ACROSS

1 Flipper, e.g.
5 Butting heads
11 W.W. II spy org.
14 Fit to serve
15 Stick together
16 Some drops
17 Spot in the top tier
19 ___ de France
20 Hot spot
21 "Nova" network
22 Not fresh
23 Without support
24 Up to, quickly
26 Rope fiber
27 "Ben-___"
28 When wadis fill
32 Pellets, e.g.
34 Speed (up)
35 Accidental occurrence
36 1941 Cary Grant tearjerker
41 It may have periods
42 Capek play
43 Church part
45 Letterhead feature
50 Burden
51 Hoodwink
52 Poetic contraction
53 Ill-suited
55 Cabinet dept. since 1965
56 Host of an annual convention attended by publishers: Abbr.
58 Hut material
59 Public-house offering
60 Measure of a company's dominance (and a literal hint to 17-, 28-, 36- and 45-Across)

64 Circle meas.
65 Cause of weird weather
66 "The heat ___!"
67 Master hand
68 Lie atop
69 Backpack item, maybe

DOWN

1 Court ploy
2 Struggling, as a pitcher
3 The Velvet Fog
4 He said "Knowledge is power"
5 Retin-A treats it
6 Poodle, perhaps
7 Startled cries
8 With all one's heart
9 Evoking an "eh"
10 Lot sights
11 Rotten to the core
12 Deal with commercially
13 It touches the Gulf of Bothnia
18 Recovered from
23 Brainstormer's cry
24 Haberdashery stock
25 2, to ½
26 Where "besuboru" is played
29 Indo-___ languages
30 He-Man's toon sister
31 Caesar's end?
33 Time to get back to work, maybe
37 Big D.C. lobby
38 One kicking oneself
39 Record collection
40 1996 Madonna role
44 Tel. no. add-on
45 Black key
46 Eyepiece
47 Got by
48 Pines
49 Spending restraints
54 Like a rare baseball game
56 Part of VISTA: Abbr.
57 Bundle up
58 Oodles
61 Emergency ___
62 Musician Brian
63 Tolkien creature

by Levi Denham

ACROSS
1 Pixels
5 Jaguars, e.g.
9 1942 movie with the song "Love Is a Song"
14 Setting for "The Plague"
15 Popular cookie
16 Each
17 Slayer of Ravana in Hindu myth
18 ___ ball
19 Aches
20 "Star Trek" genre
23 Refers (to)
24 Herald reader
28 Private line?
29 Bottom line
30 "But, ___ was ambitious, I slew him": Brutus
31 Literary oceans
33 Swinger's opportunity
34 Turntable, speakers, etc.
38 Lightly maul
39 "I've had enough!"
40 Slang expert Partridge
41 Hoosier cabinet wood
42 Lie alongside of
47 All-purpose
49 One way to win
50 Places to get online without plugging in
52 Finger ___
55 Tribe associated with the Seven Cities of Cibola
56 "That'll be the day!"
57 Zippy
58 Kind of sch.

59 Pool path
60 Breakwater
61 ___ as a blue rose
62 Mythology anthology

DOWN
1 Quai ___ (French foreign office locale)
2 Magic 8 Ball, e.g.
3 Many Sri Lankans
4 Mix-ups
5 Degree recipient
6 Sectors
7 Coastal predator
8 Romantic notes
9 Raft material
10 Marine greeting
11 Door sign
12 Snare
13 Tags

21 "Hurray for me!"
22 Marksman's skill
25 Bibliophile's citation, for short
26 At the drop of ___
27 Bottom line
29 Precious mettle?
32 Pistol, in slang
33 Early zoology topic
34 One leading a chase
35 Victor's cry
36 Turn toward sunset
37 Break for games
38 Dowel
41 Ox
43 Get up after a multiplayer football tackle
44 "Aww"

45 Largest city on Belgium's coast
46 Coca-Cola product
48 Unsafe
49 Faux pas
51 Hip activity?
52 Presidential inits.
53 Make, altogether
54 Box with a manual

by Manny Nosowsky

ACROSS
1 Lummox
8 He prophesied the destruction of Jerusalem
13 Draw
15 Its chief town is Scarborough
16 Come before
17 El Alamein battle commander
18 Cuts off the back
19 Ireland's ___ De Valera
21 Seat of White Pine County, Nev.
22 One beginning?
23 Illegal firing
24 Free of excess matter
25 Cone head?
26 Opening words of the Beatles' "We Can Work It Out"
27 Patisserie output
28 "Ditto"
29 Unlikely loser
30 Reflexologist's target
33 Ramshackle residence
34 Bombs
35 Stowe slave
36 Checked out
37 Run smoothly
40 "___ sign!"
41 Quinces, e.g.
42 It has 720 hrs.
43 You can bet on it
44 Sphere, say
45 Cry of accomplishment
46 Divider of Nebraska
48 Eh
50 Western ring
51 Pole, for one
52 Pa Clampett player on TV
53 Tile piece

DOWN
1 Book with 150 chapters
2 When two hands meet
3 Peruvian, e.g.
4 Brief bid
5 They're sometimes stacked
6 Org. that provides R.V. hookups
7 "I'll wait"
8 It has a bright side
9 Tech stock option
10 Highest peak on Africa's west coast
11 A casino may have one
12 Lama, e.g.
14 Fluctuating fortunes
15 Suffix associated with accelerators
20 Stampede sound
23 Dilettantish
24 A fifth of quinze
26 Cross
27 "Grab ___!"
28 Table in old Rome
29 Uses a tap, perhaps
30 Development area
31 50 Cent and others
32 Politely got rid of
33 Apply by repeated small touches
36 Newspaper div.
37 Impish expression of delight
38 Flap
39 Workshop of Hephaestus
41 One who handles stress effectively?
42 Galleria array
44 Novelist Barstow
45 General ___ chicken
47 Bond
49 24-Down, across the Alps

by Louis Hildebrand

ACROSS

1 Device used for film tracking shots
10 Cough up
15 "Lost in America" vehicle
16 Tickle
17 Key distributor
18 City near Dinosaur World
19 Work on a column
20 Early member of Clinton's cabinet
22 Places to serve slop
23 "The 39 Steps" star
24 Magritte's "The ___ of Man"
25 Putin foreign minister Igor ___
27 Banquet
28 Inveiglement
31 Donizetti's oeuvre
33 Wholehearted
34 Prefatory parts
35 Axes to grind
36 Straightaway
37 Pottery Barn purchases
38 1930's actress Farrell
40 ". . . ___ I again behold my Romeo!"
41 Sports Illustrated's first two-time Sportsman of the Year, 1996 and 2000
42 Plot anew
47 The two dots in "naïve"
49 Two-fisted
50 Little, bespectacled owl of the comics

51 Crossing them can affect you
53 Mote
54 Deleted
55 Grand ___
56 Says not for the first time

DOWN

1 It's full of holes
2 Add color to
3 "The scourge of the fashionable world": Schopenhauer
4 Where the malleolus is
5 Tossed over the side
6 "Oh yeah, uh-huh!"
7 Part of graduation attire

8 Everlasting
9 ___ Valley (Riverside neighbor)
10 Bother
11 Present time?
12 Does some heavy lifting
13 Plants engage in it
14 Meat quality
21 Didn't rush through
23 Kierkegaard, for one
26 Nags
27 Party platter preparer
28 Thin smoke
29 Short, of a sort
30 Juvenile outbreak
32 Sends to separate camps

33 Like some robbers' guns
34 They used to come from wells
36 Nurse's spot
39 Not leave
41 Best-seller list heading
43 Show signs of weakening
44 Hardly worth mentioning
45 Speaker of Yupik
46 Buttinskies
48 Pile of hay
49 Looks over
52 Lost, but not forgotten, in brief

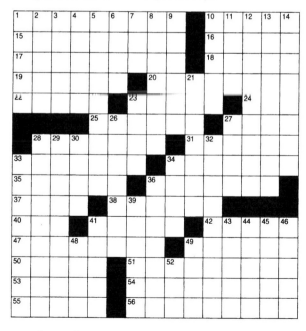

by Patrick Berry

53

ACROSS
1 Wood for Woods
5 Where to set books
10 Community service group
14 Queue
15 Four-bagger
16 Pipe problem
17 Writer Wiesel
18 Breathing
19 Unnerve
20 Hopping mad
23 Mother hog
24 Chafes
25 Tear-jerking sentiment
27 In good spirits
30 Obliterate
32 Wrestling maneuvers
33 Lose-weight-fast plan
37 Antipollution org.
38 About half of crossword clues
39 "Gotcha!"
40 Step just before publishing an article
43 Outranking
45 Sheets, tablecloths, etc.
46 Annual event at 43-Down Stadium
47 Frugality
50 Fed. watchdog since 1971
51 Motorists' org.
52 Change defeat into victory
58 Egyptian pyramids locale
60 Itinerary
61 One with a duster
62 Hawaiian strings
63 Tribal leader
64 Like good wine
65 Urge on
66 Visionaries
67 Prying

DOWN
1 Musical symbol
2 1953 Leslie Caron film
3 The "U" in I.C.U.
4 Visibly embarrassed
5 "Not too ___"
6 The 18 in a round of 18
7 Send out
8 ___ Strauss & Co.
9 Complimentary ticket
10 Santa's little helper
11 Tether
12 Musical instrument for the nonmusical
13 Distorts
21 Owned jointly by you and me
22 Sprint
26 One of the Kennedys
27 Person who's often sent compliments
28 Indian tribe with kachina dolls
29 Spirit
30 W.W. II German general Rommel
31 Sound off
33 Morse ___
34 Denny's alternative
35 Roof overhang
36 Next
38 They may sit in a glass at night
41 He could "float like a butterfly, sting like a bee"
42 Boost
43 See 46-Across
44 Ferry operator
46 Wedding helpers
47 Get ready to run, in baseball
48 Three-line poem
49 Demolishes
50 Bewhiskered swimmer
53 Film part
54 In the raw
55 Shakespearean villain
56 Fizzles out
57 Whirlpool
59 Cigar waste

by Lynn Lempel

ACROSS

1 Held a session
4 Crustaceans eaten by whales
9 Arcade flubs
14 Each
15 Kind of ink
16 Former TWA honcho Carl
17 Ill temper
18 2003 Tom Cruise movie, with "The"
20 Children's song refrain
22 Mint or chive
23 Mound dweller
24 In memoriam phrase
28 "Quién ___?" ("Who knows?"): Sp.
29 Creamsicle color
33 When doubled, a dance
36 Blue eyes or curly hair, say
39 Like many college dorms, now
40 Lean right, at sea
44 Diva's delivery
45 Copier need
46 "You, there!"
47 Hanker for
50 Greek consonants
52 What Bo-Peep did
58 RR stop
61 Workers' welfare overseer: Abbr.
62 Looie's underling
63 Van Gogh biography
67 Refinable rock
68 Put down
69 Atelier prop
70 Pa. neighbor
71 Alternative to plastic
72 Colorado's ___ Park
73 Otherworldly visitors, for short

DOWN

1 Pitchman's pitch
2 Hilltop home
3 Shoe stiffeners
4 Electrical power unit
5 Genetic letters
6 Cards with photos, for short
7 Certain print, briefly
8 Surgical beam
9 Lumberjack's call
10 Hosp. area
11 Tomb raider of film, ___ Croft
12 Comparison connector
13 Foul mood
19 Cornstarch brand
21 "___ been real!"
25 River of Aragón
26 Eat like a king
27 Snack in a shell
30 Wyle of "ER"
31 Richard of "Chicago"
32 Whirling water
33 Decked out
34 Take on
35 Sales tag words
37 "Am ___ believe . . . ?"
38 Oncle's wife
41 Follow closely
42 Paddler's target
43 NATO headquarters site
48 Housetop laborer
49 Gas brand in Canada
51 ___ Na Na
53 Birdie score, often
54 N.F.L. coach called "Papa Bear"
55 Wear down
56 "Snowy" bird
57 Suffers from sunburn
58 Retaliation for a pinch
59 Hefty horn
60 Quickly, in memos
64 China's Lao-___
65 Adherent's suffix
66 Agent's due

by Kurt Mengel and Jan-Michele Gianette

55

ACROSS

1 Auto parts giant
5 They may be vaulted
10 Sharp or flat, say
13 Does in
14 Timely benefits
15 Cap-___ (from head to foot)
16 Bureaus
19 It may have electroreceptors
20 Dances with chairs
21 Rhinestone feature
22 Gooey stuff
23 Co. that offers I.M.'s
24 It usually starts "How many . . . ?"
31 Puts out of work
32 Like "Green Acres"
33 Bushy 'do
36 Appear
37 Glass ingredient
38 "Dracula" author Stoker
39 Gunpowder, e.g.
40 Navy elite
41 Assault on Troy, e.g.
42 2003 Nicolas Cage film
45 Hood's piece
46 Sr.'s exam
47 Barely enough
50 Liquid-Plumr competitor
53 Red-white-and-blue inits.
56 Their initials can be found consecutively in 16-, 24- and 42-Across
59 Diner sign
60 1978 Peace Nobelist
61 Some mayhem
62 Common title
63 It may be skipped
64 Fair

DOWN

1 "Good one!"
2 Have a hankering
3 Floor it, with "out"
4 Long-eared equine
5 Take in
6 D
7 Soft seat
8 There are two in a loaf
9 Part of an empire up to 1991: Abbr.
10 Crude group?
11 Send packing
12 Suffix with slug
15 Win in ___ (triumph easily)
17 "___ Amore"
18 "What ___ Believes" (Doobie Brothers hit)
22 Classic 1954 sci-fi film
23 Comet competitor
24 Telephone book, essentially
25 ___ fixe
26 Flash of light
27 Husband of Bathsheba
28 Slow times
29 City of Brittany
30 Violinist Zimbalist
34 Fury
35 Straw in the wind
37 Sunnis, e.g.
38 Hog, so to speak
40 Condoleezza Rice's department
41 New England catch
43 A de Mille
44 Set off
47 ___ cell research
48 Reduce to carbon
49 Word with fine or visual
50 "Dang!"
51 Make over
52 "___ example . . ."
53 Popular computer operating system
54 "Hold everything!"
55 Concerning
57 Ltr. addenda
58 "But I heard him exclaim, ___ . . ."

by Adam G. Perl

56

ACROSS
1 Orenburg's river
5 Untouched?
9 Pond dross
13 Red Cross headquarters site
14 "Some Like __"
15 Cry of dread
16 Gulf state royalty
17 Mount Whitney's home
19 Nancy, in Nancy
20 Formicide: ant:: pulicide: __
21 __ Hirsch of "Lords of Dogtown"
22 1950's–60's twangy guitarist
25 Skating competition
27 Name in a Shakespearean title
28 Responses to tattooers
30 Something that's bruisable
31 Started (off)
32 Item at center stage
34 Hudson River city
35 Singer with a 1962 #1 hit that started a dance craze (and a hint to this puzzle's theme)
38 Stain blockers
41 It may be free for philosophers
42 "Dream on!"
45 "Ti __" (Casanova's declaration)
46 Stay-at-home __
47 Head of a flock
49 Froth
51 Aft
54 "The Brady Bunch" housekeeper
56 Extirpate, with "out"
57 1983 Indy winner Tom
58 Button holders
60 Much of Us Weekly
61 Smart
62 Come (from)
63 Long, long time
64 Interjects
65 Concert highlight
66 Something that's bruisable

DOWN
1 Where the shilling is money
2 Get back on
3 Enliven
4 Actor Burton
5 Kept in a pen
6 Each
7 Postal motto conjunction
8 To be, overseas
9 The merry widow, in the 1934 musical "The Merry Widow"
10 "Gigi" co-star
11 Experience
12 Bygone bird
14 The __ Brothers of R & B
18 Hearing aids?
20 Gucci rival
23 Seasonal songs
24 Hayseed
26 __ sauce
29 Prekindergarten
32 Crete's highest peak: Abbr.
33 "__ wait"
34 Electric dart shooter
36 Its slogan used to be "One mission. Yours."
37 Restaurant employee
38 What hist. majors pursue
39 Stuck
40 Broad way
43 "Take this job and shove it!"
44 Betrothed
46 Art style, informally
47 Went with
48 Deep fissure
50 Hands, slangily
52 Come in second
53 Classic sculpture
55 Spanish form of "to be" after "tú"
58 Test-conducting org.
59 __-Magnon
60 Neighbor of Iran: Abbr.

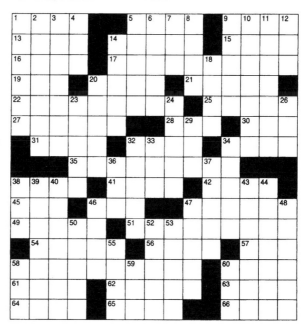

by Bonnie L. Gentry

ACROSS

1 Where Patrick Ewing was born
8 Jalapeño-topped snack
14 Raising hell
15 Parry
16 Get out of shape?
17 Tranquilizer
18 Little butter?
19 Got a feel for, in a way
21 Counter offer
22 Denial
24 Wonder-full sounds
25 Kind of PC command
26 Pet dog at Camp Swampy
27 Giotto and others
29 Splitting words
31 Jacques Chirac and Grover Cleveland, once
32 Peripherals
34 Rosetta stone composition
38 Salt, sometimes
42 Desi's daughter
43 Portrays precisely
47 Grammy-nominated Franklin
48 An admission of guilt
49 Actor Willard of "The Color Purple"
50 ___ Canals
51 Shake alternative
52 Patterned fabrics
54 Certain dama: Abbr.
56 Staked out, say
58 Apt to snap back?
60 They may be required to get in

61 Supermarket checkout staple
62 Pickles
63 Soul-searching sessions?

DOWN

1 Enthusiast, informally
2 Divinely chosen
3 Ruled
4 Counselor: Abbr.
5 The "I" in I. M. Pei
6 Mailing label words
7 Medium
8 Sine qua non
9 The Titans were in it: Abbr.
10 Sociological study
11 Series of six
12 Leopardus pardalis
13 Cause of some fractures
15 Fancy
20 Hedda's schoolmate in "Hedda Gabler"
23 Frequent losers and gainers
25 Storybook ending, sometimes
26 Costa Rica's ___ Peninsula
28 Ear part
30 Put ___ to
33 Prussian pronoun
35 Psalm 119, e.g.
36 Trip in a tux, maybe
37 Picker-upper
39 Some roasters
40 Holder of notions
41 "Sorry!"
43 Chinatown chow choice
44 Go by
45 Monet subject
46 Table
52 Fashionable group
53 It takes quite a while to tell
55 Components of good deals
57 Randomizer
59 Star

by Elizabeth C. Gorski

58

ACROSS
1 Agape, say
5 Poor
15 ___ room
16 Comment after a setup
17 See 57-Across
18 Features of standardized tests
19 Farm area
20 Long
21 Farm area
22 Like some injuries
24 Sweet drink
27 Takes in
28 Song in "The Sound of Music"
29 Lucky ones, it's said
30 NBC Sports personality
34 Front
35 Musician's better half
36 Golfer Michelle
37 Scrambler's aid
40 Place for old get-togethers
42 Terror's opposite
43 Like some traffic
44 Heat-seeking missile
47 Vacate a position, informally
48 Wait in line
49 Belted
50 A little birdie
51 Foreglimpse
55 Missing the boat
56 Movement explainer
57 With 17-Across, big name in international news
58 Watched
59 Rocky peaks

DOWN
1 Plays the innocent one
2 "Bo-o-oring"
3 Relaxing
4 Shakes
5 Protests
6 Catcher Buck ___, elected to baseball's Hall of Fame in its first year
7 Amounted (to)
8 Full of: Suffix
9 Patriots' org.
10 Soft & ___
11 Shelters on the beach
12 Firenze friends
13 Prefix with fluoride
14 Big flop
20 Core
23 H.M.O. listings
24 Log tossed in competition
25 Sea predator
26 "Notorious" setting, 1946
28 Tahoe or Monterey
30 Canine, e.g.
31 Words said while clapping
32 Wannabe rocker's instrument
33 Abalone eaters
35 Learned
38 Old western villain
39 University dept.
40 Having words
41 Right-thinking grp.
43 Slick
44 Goes over
45 Belief
46 Bisected
47 Instrument accompanying a tambura
49 Festive
52 Post office letters
53 Having one sharp
54 Sch. in the Big Ten
55 Wasted

by Joe DiPietro

ACROSS

1 Put up, as a picture
5 ___ salts
10 Restaurant acronym
14 Fit for drafting
15 Mamma's mate
16 Shore bird
17 Headliner
18 Strand, as during a blizzard
19 Give a nudge, so to speak
20 "Take a chill pill"
23 CD predecessors
24 Conservative pundit Alan
25 Old copy machine, briefly
28 Pea's place
29 Exams for future attys.
33 Female in a flock
34 Whistle-blower on a court
35 Error
36 Out of it, as a boxer
40 Embedded
41 Witch
42 Stephen of "The Crying Game"
43 When some news airs
44 Like hearts and diamonds
45 Great time
47 Treated a lawn, perhaps
49 Winning tic-tac-toe row
50 Finally accept
57 Gave the boot
58 Pep up
59 Wax-coated cheese
60 Big rig
61 Singer Lopez
62 El ___ (Pacific Ocean phenomenon)
63 Ship's speed unit
64 Tennis champ Monica
65 Recipients of the cries seen at the starts of 20-, 36- and 50-Across and 7-Down

DOWN

1 "Bonanza" son
2 Opposed to
3 In order
4 Scramble, as a signal
5 Grand stories
6 Small indentation
7 "We were just talking about you"
8 Voiced a view
9 1975 Barry Manilow #1 hit
10 "Sure, why not"
11 Toss
12 Gymnast Korbut
13 Common movie house name ending
21 G.I.'s address
22 Excavation find
25 TV, radio, etc.
26 Words of refusal
27 Whimpers
28 Word before capita or annum
30 Integra maker
31 Adjusts, as a piano
32 Went after
34 Reel's partner
35 Ryan of "When Harry Met Sally"
37 Performed a routine perfectly
38 Mr. ___
39 Ate
44 Stop working at 65, say
45 Baseball's Jackson and others
46 Bargain-basement
48 Drops feathers
49 Old Dodges
50 Wine holder
51 Field team
52 Quick note
53 Philosopher Descartes
54 Peculiar: Prefix
55 Powdered drink mix
56 Med. care choices

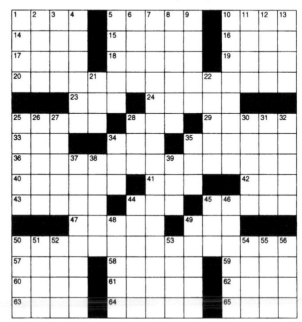

by Jim Hyres

60

ACROSS
1 "Jaywalker" of late-night TV
5 C sharp equivalent
10 __ Spumante
14 Worse than bad
15 Something coffee has
16 Golda of Israel
17 Leaves for cooking
18 About 39 inches
19 Scottish hillside
20 Coming attractions shot at a mobile home park?
23 It may be passed on the Hill
25 __ Speedwagon
26 __ work (road sign)
27 Full-length films shot at a day spa?
32 To any extent
33 Chafes
34 Lariat
35 Late civil rights pioneer Rosa
37 Gillette razor
41 "__ on Down the Road"
42 Throat malady
43 Film segments shot at an arsenal?
48 Ice cream sundae, e.g.
49 Eggs
50 Anka's "__ Beso"
51 Documentaries shot at a vacation paradise?
56 Did laps, say
57 Modern reading material
58 "Sorry about that!"
61 Fountain of jazz
62 Water ride
63 Expert
64 Iditarod entry
65 Like most manuscripts
66 On

DOWN
1 French article
2 "Deliver Us From __," 2003 film
3 Nip before a tuck?
4 Table spread
5 Interest of a knight in shining armor
6 Without
7 Trent of the Senate
8 From the U.S.
9 Skater Lipinski
10 English novelist Eric
11 Unruffled
12 Jeweled coronets
13 "__ my case"
21 River to the Caspian
22 Don of morning radio
23 Many miles away
24 Roman statesman and writer
28 Spot of land in the Seine
29 Goofed
30 Diving bird
31 Superstation letters
35 Scorecard number
36 "__ was saying"
37 U.S./Eur. divider
38 Auditions
39 Counts in the gym
40 Lhasa __ (dog)
41 Words to Brutus
42 Surgery reminder
43 Embroidery yarn
44 Make fizzy
45 Rear-ended, e.g.
46 "Beat it!"
47 Brought forth
48 Kitchen measures: Abbr.
52 Skillful
53 Skillfully
54 Egg drop, e.g.
55 "Animal House" attire
59 For
60 "How's it hangin', bro?"

by Sarah Keller

ACROSS

1 Crop up
6 Service leader
11 Cricket club
14 Like some eclipses
15 Detective Pinkerton
16 "___ you sure?"
17 Amphitheater cover?
19 Contest of sorts
20 Sharp as a tack
21 Macadam ingredient
22 O'Neal of "Peyton Place"
23 Temperamental sort
25 Pitchfork features
27 Gore and Hirt
30 Coins found at a dig?
34 Takes off
36 Genetic letters
37 Engine unit
38 Swarm member
39 Spa offering
42 Lee of Marvel Comics
43 Packed away
45 Prospector's need
46 Julia's role in "Ocean's Twelve"
47 Prefight ceremony?
51 A.A.R.P. part: Abbr.
52 Overthrow, e.g.
53 Dirty look
55 Deimos orbits it
57 ___ Irvin, who designed the first cover for The New Yorker
59 On the hook
63 William Tell's canton
64 Calm at a wrestling match?

66 Pewter, in part
67 "___ World Turns"
68 Children's refrain
69 Put out
70 Questionnaire category
71 Played over

DOWN

1 Thomas ___ Edison
2 Wishes undone
3 J., F. or K.: Abbr.
4 Tijuana toast
5 Like the Kama Sutra
6 No-goodnik
7 Came to rest on a wire, e.g.
8 Sounds during wool-shearing
9 East Los Angeles, e.g.
10 Helpful contacts
11 Saturday night hire, often
12 Field
13 11-Down, frequently
18 They're dangerous when they're high
22 Stand up to
24 Ballerina Pavlova
26 Pro Bowl org.
27 Tattered Tom's creator
28 Maui neighbor
29 Little bit
31 Hose shade
32 Get on
33 Surrealist Max
35 Has the tiller
40 Picture holder
41 San ___, Tex.
44 Bergen's locale: Abbr.
48 Ranger's domain
49 Year-end decoration
50 Cow that hasn't had a cow
54 Flaxlike fiber
55 Kennel club rejectee
56 Star turn
58 Need an ice bag
60 Schooner filler
61 Luke Skywalker's sister
62 School on the Thames
64 Kung ___ chicken
65 Suffix with auction

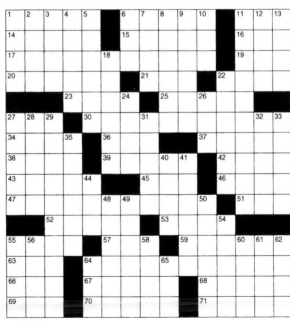

by Randall J. Hartman

62

ACROSS

1 Kind of gun
4 Catalyzing subatomic particles
9 Singe
13 Father of octuplets on "The Simpsons"
14 Picture to carry around?
16 Knock over
17 Clowns' wear
18 Pipe fitting
19 O.T. book
20 It has many pages
21 Skull and Bones member, e.g.
22 Receivers of manumission
25 Dobbin's "right"
26 Cape ___, Portugal (continental Europe's westernmost point)
28 Pocket filler
30 Link
31 Flashlight backup
36 Title for this puzzle
40 Brunch option
41 About
44 "___ I Can Make It on My Own" (Tammy Wynette #1 hit)
45 Grade schooler's reward
46 German pronoun
47 Animal that can be ridden
51 Soprano Marton
52 Not tied up, as funds
56 Ring of plumerias
57 Like Duroc hogs
58 Leader in sports
61 Put the kibosh on
62 Makeup carrier
63 Set
64 CPR deliverers
65 Wedding reception party?
66 Emerson's "___ to Beauty"

DOWN

1 Rushed headlong
2 Mission commemorated on the back of the Eisenhower dollar coin
3 Subject of annual Congressional budget debate
4 ___-Argonne offensive of W.W. I
5 Open, in a way
6 Gambling inits.
7 Highlands negative
8 Camera types, for short
9 "Shake a leg!"
10 Takes one's turn
11 Threshold for the Vienna Boys' Choir
12 Switch in the tournament schedule, maybe
14 Scans ordered by M.D.'s
15 Suffix with glass
23 Adipocyte
24 Fretted instrument
27 Words with thumb or bum
29 Car making a return trip?
30 Storage units
32 Sweet drink
33 Like staples
34 Tylenol alternative
35 Canyon area
37 Holmes to Conan Doyle, e.g.
38 Like soda crackers
39 Not choose one side or the other
41 Lead-in to a questionable opinion
42 Two bells in the forenoon watch
43 Freshly worded
48 Pool problem
49 Reagan attorney general
50 Leeds's river
53 Gremlins and others, for short
54 Little, in Leith
55 "A Wild ___" (cartoon in which Bugs Bunny first says "What's up, Doc?")
59 60's war zone
60 U. of Md. is in it

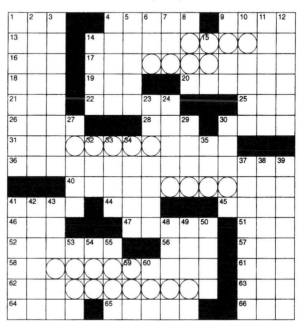

by Byron Walden

ACROSS

1 Sing, in a way
10 ___ Court (London district)
15 How campers may sit
16 Blocks
17 Say something personally embarrassing
19 Commemorative piece
20 Concerts
21 Suffix with señor
23 Mole
24 Scottish Peace Nobelist John Boyd ___
27 Seine tributary
29 Bones, anatomically
33 It's written with acid
38 Popular Florida amusement park
39 Let hang
40 Oxford foundation?
41 Over the hill, maybe
42 Film director Russell
43 African capital
47 Darn
49 Power structure
52 Bag carrier
56 Got in
60 Chosen
61 Second class, perhaps
62 Jug
63 Do-or-die effort

DOWN

1 Barely catches
2 "Sometimes you feel like ___ . . ."
3 Pal
4 Digestive bacteria
5 Long odds
6 Not just look
7 Intro providers
8 ___-locks (tangled hair)
9 1988 Olympics site
10 Like some kitchens
11 Originator of the maxim "One swallow does not make a summer"
12 Civil War general Jesse
13 Rested
14 Retired fleet
18 ___ hunch
22 Reply to "You're a stinker!"
23 Eyes
24 Girasols
25 Megabucks event?
26 Try to beat
28 Had a quick turn
30 Was really awful
31 Smarts
32 "As You Like It" setting
34 Kind of package
35 Dix preceder
36 Old Apple computers
37 Strong brews
44 Rocky ridge
45 Nonfunctioning
46 Ever
48 "Rome ___ . . ."
49 Gets on
50 Insect organ
51 Brighton landmark
53 Actress Talbot
54 Hamlet's big brother
55 Give ___ to (acknowledge)
57 Goddess, to Gaius
58 Workload for eds.
59 Suffix with special

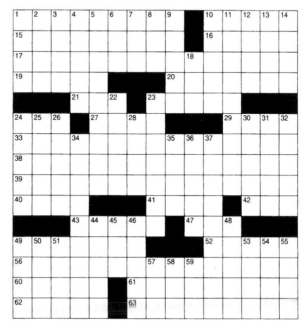

by Martin Ashwood-Smith

64

ACROSS

1 Superman feature
9 Wood work
15 Tiny openings
16 Designate
17 Petition for again
18 Teacher at TV's James Buchanan High
19 Unmanly
20 Love handle?
21 Blueblood line
22 Classic 1950 film presented mostly in flashback
23 Like some knots
26 Adlai Stevenson's middle name
27 N.H.L. defenseman who twice led the league in scoring
29 Aquarium implement
30 Exclamation added to the O.E.D. in 2001
33 One hanging around the kitchen
34 Grill refuse
35 Game whose name players yell during play
36 Daniel who played Furillo
39 Place for a needle
41 Period following Rome's fall
44 It has hooks
46 Like the sun god Inti
48 Stops daydreaming
49 1950's–60's sex symbol's nickname

51 Time on a marquee
52 Wrigglers, e.g.
53 Menu option
54 Invitation for a radio call-in
55 Prepare for a second crop
56 Was a neighbor of

DOWN

1 Bout of indulgence
2 Tin, maybe
3 First name in Indian politics
4 Antitheft device
5 Returns after being out
6 ___-Ude (Asian capital)

7 Physician Laënnec, who invented the stethoscope
8 The U.S. banned it in 1967
9 Babas and babkas
10 Unsatisfied person's request
11 "I'm busy!"
12 Something a pumpkin can provide
13 Radially symmetric sea creatures
14 Head count of an army
20 California observatory
22 Duracell rival
24 Structural support

25 Medium that uses ten-codes
28 Row
30 Parking lot sight
31 Private meeting
32 Roller derby wear
36 Museum official
37 Concluding part
38 Base
40 Business magnate's holdings
42 Iced treat
43 Liquid in a drip
45 Cowboy's companion
47 Illustrious
49 T'ang dynasty poet
50 State categorically
52 High ball

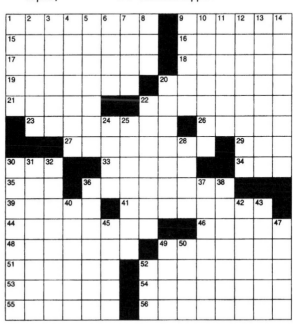

by Patrick Berry

ACROSS

1 Tiff
5 Go out on the ocean
9 Bogged down
14 Letter before kappa
15 Longest river of Spain
16 "___ fired" (Trump catchphrase)
17 Classic holiday entertainment
20 In whatever way
21 Swing that rips the leather off the ball
22 "Waking ___ Devine" (1998 film)
23 Co. photo badges, e.g.
24 W.W. II female
26 Expectorate
28 Houston major-leaguer
30 Crouches
34 Amo, amas, ___ . . .
37 Morays
39 Dickens's ___ Heep
40 Shock
43 Three to one, e.g.
44 Nick and ___ Charles of "The Thin Man"
45 44-Across's dog
46 Lagoons' surroundings
48 Sleek fabric
50 "Too bad!"
52 Mos. and mos.
53 Clemson competes in it: Abbr.
56 Fit ___ fiddle
59 Horse feed
61 20 Questions category

63 "The Thin Man," for one
66 Bygone airline
67 Corner chesspiece
68 Sacked out
69 Sound made while sacked out
70 I's
71 Chess ending

DOWN

1 Biblical mount
2 Hit with a hammer
3 Lawyers: Abbr.
4 Dashboard dial, for short
5 Brine
6 Network of "Lost"
7 Nettles
8 Many movie houses
9 Magical aura
10 Letters of debt
11 Undo
12 Art Deco master
13 Monopoly card
18 Has the oars
19 Emulates Eminem
25 King of Thebes, in myth
27 Headdress that's wound
28 Head of the Huns
29 Actor Edward James ___
31 Is under the weather
32 Stretched tight
33 Queens stadium
34 Magician's opening
35 Castle protector
36 Choir voice
38 Leave the straight and narrow
41 Leader's cry, said with a wave
42 Where to hang derbies and fedoras
47 Volvo rival
49 "But there ___ joy in Mudville . . ."
51 Look steadily
53 Itsy-bitsy creature
54 West Pointer
55 Bonnie's partner in crime
56 Nile slitherers
57 Good, close look
58 Florence's river
60 Walk with difficulty
62 Mosque V.I.P.
64 Hearing aid
65 British john

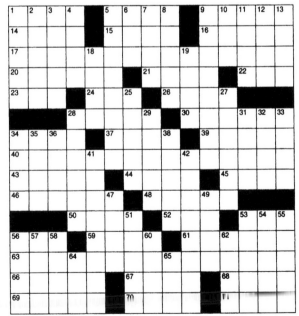

by Jay Livingston

66

ACROSS
1 Poisonous plants
7 Letters for Letterman
10 "Right now!"
14 Discordant
15 Cry heard in a bullring
16 Small jet maker
17 Place to test aerodynamics
19 Isaac's eldest
20 Bakery gizmo
21 One of the Lennons
22 Broadway background
23 Hoopster Archibald
24 Kukla or Ollie, e.g.
28 Give it a go
30 Employ more employees
31 Glass marble
34 Clutch
37 Chinese author ___ Yutang
38 Placing (and a hint to the first words of 17-, 24-, 47- and 60-Across)
41 Stool pigeon
42 Out of style
43 Dull drills
44 2,000 pounds
46 Telepathic letters
47 Skinny Minnie
51 Funnyman Sandler
55 Offbeat
56 Some shortening
57 Brazilian soccer legend
58 Amorphous mass
60 Author's success
62 "La Bohème" heroine
63 Bit of sunshine

64 Practical
65 Direction wagon trains headed
66 Alias
67 Nebraska river

DOWN
1 Greeted, as the New Year
2 Central New York city
3 "Water Lilies" painter
4 Mario of the Indianapolis 500
5 Hipster
6 Like half-melted snow
7 Arthur ___ Doyle
8 It's not 100% this or that
9 French seasoning
10 Is in dreamland
11 Aviator in search of bugs
12 Battery size
13 Robert Morse Tony-winning role
18 PBS benefactor
22 Potluck get-togethers
25 Face, slangily
26 Some cyber-reading
27 Looks after
29 Give an answer
31 60's–70's dos
32 Goliath
33 Vestibules
34 Dogfaces
35 Hosp. staffers
36 Count of candles on a cake
39 "___ in there!"
40 Come to terms for less jail time, say

45 Gossip unit
46 Ultimately becomes
48 Dickens's "___ House"
49 Cushy course
50 Know-how
52 Blue-and-white earthenware
53 Alaskan native
54 Singer Haggard
58 Upscale auto initials
59 Practice tact, perhaps
60 Playtex offering
61 Immigrant's subj.

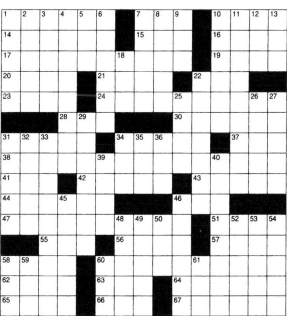

by Gail Grabowski and Nancy Salomon

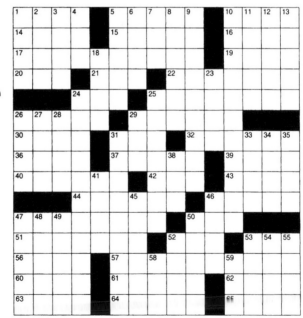

67

ACROSS

1 See 24-Down
5 Easy ___
10 Mental keenness
14 Nebraska native
15 Unlikely to defect
16 "The Plague" city
17 Bandleader known for 55-Down
19 Seine feeder
20 Many Tyson finishes
21 Capek play
22 "Gullible's Travels" writer
24 URL ending
25 Cemetery, informally
26 Up
29 Judd of "Taxi"
30 Vestments, e.g.
31 Big jerk
32 1926 Channel swimmer
36 Suffix with psych-
37 Open, in a way
39 Start of many Hope/Crosby film titles
40 Philippine locale in W.W. II
42 ___ Gratia Artis
43 A bunch of
44 Absorbed, in a way
46 Krone spenders
47 Zigged and zagged
50 Door sign
51 Conestoga driver
52 Guff
53 Atlantic City mecca, with "the"
56 "Vidi," translated
57 Bandleader known for 47-Down

60 St. Petersburg's river
61 Kegger wear, maybe
62 "Mockingbird" singer Foxx
63 Colored like a certain hound
64 Blow hard
65 Daimler partner

DOWN

1 Varsity letter earner
2 Words of agreement
3 Part of R.S.V.P.
4 Poetic contraction
5 Vinyl collectible
6 Go parasailing
7 Cries of regret
8 Entruster of property
9 Under-the-sink items
10 Bandleader known for 25-Down
11 "Three Sisters" sister
12 Stun gun
13 Bergen dummy
18 Fox or turkey follower
23 Invoice abbr.
24 Bandleader known for 1-Across
25 See 10-Down
26 "A Girl, a Guy and ___" (1941 Ball movie)
27 "Later"
28 Old chap, say
29 Barbarous one
31 Lunch counter orders

33 Horse coloring
34 Pool path
35 Breyers rival
38 Verb with thou
41 Interminable time
45 Transplant
46 Johnny who played Willy Wonka
47 See 57-Across
48 Surgery tool
49 Tequila source
50 The "Divine" Bette
52 Cry in a mudslinging contest
53 Trident part
54 Call from the flock
55 See 17-Across
58 Actor Tognazzi
59 Thorax protector

by Ed Early

ACROSS

1 It may wash out bridges and embankments (as in this puzzle)
6 Onetime White House scandal
10 Salt source
13 Afghan's neighbor
14 Secure
15 Scotland Yard discovery
17 Honey bunch?
18 Actress with an uncredited part in "Zoolander"
20 Bedazzles
22 Get to, in a way
23 Common ___
24 In case this is of interest . . .
25 With 49-Across, famous line from "The Rime of the Ancient Mariner"
31 Not just swallow
35 City NW of Orlando
36 Depraved
37 Item that may be "Miss" printed?
38 Ingredient in a Caribbean cocktail
39 Took a pleasure excursion
42 Visit Sundance, maybe
43 One of Charlie's Angels
45 Covered walk
46 Large vocal group
48 Cuarto de baño, e.g.
49 See 25-Across
51 Field of note?: Abbr.
53 The difference between regular mail and e-mail?
54 Batter's hope
57 Canon composer
63 Bialy, e.g.
65 "Me, too"
66 Distinguish
67 Craft that pulled over for Sirens
68 Old World relative of a canary
69 It's springless
70 Source of a stream
71 Hydrogeologist's concern

DOWN

1 Hooch
2 Hubbard of Scientology
3 Kiln
4 Like a short film
5 Chaos
6 Big inits. in car financing
7 Top-of-the-line
8 A gazillion
9 Before, in poetry
10 Panoramic photos, say
11 Pizazz
12 Rocket scientist's prefix
16 Canal, e.g.
19 "___ I?"
21 Hillbilly's negative
24 Sovereign
25 Tears, metaphorically
26 TSX maker
27 Sri Lankan tongue
28 "Boston Legal" broadcaster
29 Lake divided by a state line
30 Spanish 101 verb
32 Rush
33 Glacial deposit
34 Onetime White House scandal
40 "___ Death" ("Peer Gynt" piece)
41 Maine
44 When repeated, a response to "What's new?"
47 A Clinton
50 Derisive cry
52 Egyptian tomb item
54 Big trouble
55 Apartment next to a super, maybe
56 Distance between some posts
57 Look (over)
58 Tiny pond-dweller
59 Knucklehead
60 Caustic comment
61 Runner Zátopek
62 Main
64 Big cheer

by Lee Glickstein and Craig Kasper

ACROSS
1 Journalist's get
6 South extension
9 Jerk
14 Participants get a kick out of it
15 Eastern path
16 Worcester university
17 Last word?
18 Workout follower
20 Alpha Orionis
22 Stamp of approval?
23 Like some potatoes or oysters
25 112.5°
28 Commuting choices
29 Bloody Mary sings it
33 $10,000,000 award won in 2004 for successful private space flight
35 Old treasure transporters
36 "Alias" character Derevko
37 Taken
38 "Behold, the people ___": Genesis 11:6
39 Officially approved
41 R & B singer Phillips
42 C_2H_5OH
43 ___ juris
44 Dismiss
45 Indemnify
48 Neighbor of Slough
51 "A Confession" author
55 Mary Lily one
57 Bracketed material
58 Very big
59 Temporal stretch
60 Air Force Ones, e.g.
61 Canonized Catalan
62 One with drill skill: Abbr.
63 Voltaire's faith

DOWN
1 Evidence of injury
2 Computer programmer's work
3 Tending to the matter
4 Some moldings
5 Pablo Picasso's "one and only master"
6 A Rosenberg and others
7 "The Thief of Baghdad" director Walsh
8 Fair
9 Jr.'s place
10 Most gray, in a way
11 Equivocates
12 Noted member of a Hollywood stable
13 Food that may be pickled
19 Perianth part
21 It might make waves
24 Ferry destination from Liberty State Park
25 Drive out, in a way
26 Sail extender
27 Novelist Remarque
30 Flutter
31 Incorporate
32 River near Albertville
34 Seriously
35 Flit
37 Ready for battle, say
40 Agronomists' study
41 Prefix with pop
43 Hindu precepts
46 Word after cutting and running
47 "Ah, Wilderness!" mother
48 Those caballeros
49 One with a big bell
50 Crack ___
52 Polynesian carving
53 Some tributes
54 Backwoods assent
56 Hudson contemporary

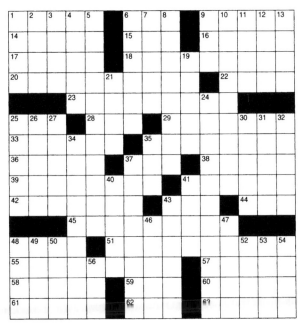

by Eric Berlin

70

ACROSS
1 Part of a French court
4 Drift
8 Scattered
14 "___ Box" (1992 six-disc set)
15 Hit man
16 Hot
17 Russian news source
19 "A Man Must Fight" author Gene
20 Couples
21 Starter: Abbr.
22 Kitchen gadgets
23 Kinship
26 Govt. loan agency
27 Looking up
28 When "77 Sunset Strip" aired: Abbr.
31 What a prosecutor may try to prove
34 ___ for iron
35 Presidential middle name
36 Locale called Minnahannock by the Algonquin Indians, bought by the Dutch in 1637
39 Popular syrup
40 Make tracks?
41 Loquacious
42 Short
43 Leaves alone
45 River connected to a 165-mile long European canal
46 Psyched about going
49 Military craft
52 Slutty
53 Villain at Crab Key fortress
55 The only royal palace in the U.S.
56 "My view is . . ."
58 Big name in oil
59 Opposite of "No, no"
60 Little wriggler
61 Hit list?
62 Abbr. before a date
63 "The Matrix" hero

DOWN
1 That's an order
2 Expand, as a compressed file
3 Alibi
4 Mich. neighbor
5 When to hear "O Romeo, Romeo! wherefore art thou Romeo?"
6 Puts on a show
7 Eagle's place
8 Nonessential
9 Like a mai tai
10 Picture
11 "A Different Read on Life" magazine
12 One holding a ball, maybe
13 ___ Grand (supermarket brand)
18 1962 hit with the lyric "Kiss me mucho"
24 Wainscot section
25 Newton, for one
28 Computer option
29 Bluster
30 1981 adventure film hero
31 Bugs
32 Ancient mariner?
33 Broadcaster
35 Dessert style
37 Squeezed
38 "Fer ___!"
43 Occult practice
44 Sci-fi preservation technique
46 Outdoor party
47 Percy Bysshe Shelley, e.g.
48 Airport no-no
49 Pre-Celtic person
50 Deere competitor
51 Brief interruption
54 One of the Ringling Brothers
57 Naughty boy, in "Toy Story"

by Karen M. Tracey

71

ACROSS
1 All excited
5 Unexpected sports outcome
10 Small salamander
14 Earring site
15 John who was once known as the Teflon Don
16 "That's clear"
17 Houston Astro, for one
19 Stare
20 Met production
21 Chart toppers
23 Dot-com's address
25 Ump's call
26 Actors not playing major parts
34 "Quiet, please!"
35 Disdain
36 Father Christmas
37 Sounds of relief
39 Keep after
41 ___ Piper
42 Bad way to run
44 Pigpens
46 Caribbean, e.g.
47 In the driver's seat
50 What to call an officer, maybe
51 Hither's partner
52 Where to get taxis
58 Comparison shopper's quest
62 Norway's capital
63 Not bad in result
65 Mix (up)
66 Laser printer powder
67 Diva Horne
68 Spinning toys
69 Winter falls
70 Historic periods

DOWN
1 Brand for Fido
2 Trail mix
3 Double-reed instrument
4 Get ready
5 "Yuck!"
6 Experts in vote-getting
7 Flower stalk
8 Jazz singer James
9 Attaches, as a rope
10 Bedtime drink
11 Actor Morales
12 Cried
13 Golf ball props
18 Field protectors
22 Holds close
24 ___ Ness monster
26 "Naughty, naughty!"
27 "Yeah"
28 Perch
29 It's a fact
30 Navel type
31 Biscotti flavoring
32 Girder material
33 "I did it!"
34 Swedish auto
38 Tailor's tool
40 Wet, as morning grass
43 Make a sweater
45 Rudely push
48 Pre-edited versions
49 Allow
52 Purchase price
53 Regarding
54 Radar image
55 It follows 11
56 First 007 film
57 One-dish meal
59 Suggestive look
60 School for a future ens.
61 J.F.K. postings
64 Mins. and mins.

by Marjorie Berg

ACROSS

1 Showman Ziegfeld
4 Shakespearean character who calls himself "a very foolish fond old man"
8 Traveler's baggage handler
14 Mary's boss on "The Mary Tyler Moore Show"
15 Writer Sarah ___ Jewett
16 Bogged down
17 Beer festival mo.
18 Musical staff symbol
19 Wanderers
20 Nickname for author Ernest
23 Prunes, once
24 France's Belle-___
25 Vegetarian's protein source
28 Abominable Snowman
29 Classic New York City eatery
32 Amtrak facility: Abbr.
34 Cartoonist Drake
35 Summer along the Seine
36 Paul McCartney in the Beatles
40 Not in stock yet
42 "So that's it!"
43 Milne's "The House at ___ Corner"
45 Anka's "___ Beso"
46 Fanny Brice radio character
49 Burst of wind
53 Greek peak
54 Card below quattro
55 Postal scale marking
56 This puzzle's theme

60 Photo assignments
62 "It's ___" ("I'm buying")
63 A couple of chips, maybe
64 Dawn goddess
65 ___ Martin (cognac brand)
66 Brenda of country music
67 Geological wonder
68 Madrid Mmes.
69 Wind up

DOWN

1 Disk type
2 Place
3 Yield
4 Scottish boating spots
5 ___ Stanley Gardner

6 What Procrit may treat
7 Uses another roll on
8 Symbol of troth
9 Sufficient, in poetry
10 Ex-senator Alfonse
11 Filled in a coloring book
12 I.R.S. exam: Abbr.
13 Sour cream container amts.
21 Not quite right
22 "Super!"
26 Big bash
27 ___-friendly
29 Lawyer created by 5-Down
30 Areas between shoulders?
31 Slugger Slaughter
33 Rewards for waiting

36 Popular clown at kids' parties
37 Teachers like to hear them
38 Long, drawn-out excuse
39 One end of a bridge
41 Scoundrel
44 "Egad!"
47 Louts
48 More acute
50 Not up to it
51 Sift
52 Tried out
55 Minds
57 To be, to Henri
58 Boris Godunov, e.g.
59 Madame Bovary
60 Droop
61 Ruby or emerald

by Sarah Keller

ACROSS

1 Spin doctor's concern
6 Mediterranean spewer
10 Sobriquet for Haydn
14 Gabbed away
15 Not fer
16 Drive away, as a thief?
17 With 21-Across, there's no . . .
19 Fall shade
20 Joanne of westerns
21 See 17-Across
23 Hard to miss
27 Sings in the Alps
28 Taters
29 It may be hard on a construction worker
32 Alley button
33 Dish served with a lemon wedge
34 Good source of potassium
36 There's no . . .
41 Brought up
42 "Little" boy of early comics
44 Bring a smile to
48 ___ Lingus
49 Take it off, take it all off
50 Shiny cotton fabric
52 "Told ya!"
54 With 59-Across, there's no . . .
57 "___ we there yet?"
58 School with King's Scholars
59 See 54-Across
64 Tabula ___
65 Asian princess

66 Company that took over Reynolds Metals in 2000
67 Lousy eggs?
68 Quartz type
69 Former Japanese capital

DOWN

1 Lyricist Gershwin
2 Raincoat, for short
3 Mandela's org.
4 "Sure, why not?!"
5 Accustoms
6 Bother, with "at"
7 Abbreviation said with a "Whew!"
8 Bogotá boy
9 Steamed
10 Memorial Day event
11 Takes advantage of, say
12 Mortar's partner
13 Swear (to)
18 Taker of vows
22 Service reading
23 Pressure cooker's sound
24 Each, slangily
25 Break in the action
26 Comedian's Muse
30 Licorice-scented herb
31 "Any ___?"
34 Arthur of "The Golden Girls"
35 ABC newsman Potter
37 Angler's basket
38 Sneakily

39 Trifling
40 Namer of a representative to OPEC, maybe
43 Unlock, to a poet
44 Rearward
45 Drink made with curaçao
46 Maximum
47 Interpreted to be
49 Run of luck
51 Funny-car fuel
53 Something that may be seen in a bank
55 Genghis ___
56 Start of a kid's counting rhyme
60 Fotos
61 Prefix with friendly
62 "___ so!"
63 The way of the Chinese

by Philip Thomson

ACROSS
1 Semifluid material
6 Enchantress, in Shakespeare
9 Put a belt on
13 Why and wherefore
15 Prefix with logical
16 "Old" ship's name
17 Big name in printers
18 2005 Samuel L. Jackson biopic
20 George who wrote "Fables in Slang"
21 De bene ___ (legal phrase)
22 Preoccupy
23 Controlled
24 Recording medium, for short
25 Humorist Shriner
26 Go through
28 Many a stained glass window
31 Eyelashes
32 Same old, same old
36 Without a break
37 Time in advertising
38 Knocked on the noggin
40 Mineral suffix
41 28-Across, e.g.
44 Some notes
45 Lap again
48 Foreign dignitary
49 "The Lord of the Rings" extra
50 Ones getting Secret Service protection
52 Acronym since 1941

54 Private talks
55 Bud protector
56 Uncover
57 Innocence locale
58 Some job hunters: Abbr.
59 University of Maryland, informally

DOWN
1 Going for, with "at"
2 "Domani" singer Julius
3 Wedding reception cry
4 Because
5 Do slam-dancing
6 Really enjoyed oneself
7 A's, e.g.
8 Beau ___

9 Dental problem
10 "Wow!"
11 Land that declared its independence on 11/11/1965
12 Words said before shaking hands
14 Ratatouille ___
15 Hound, say
19 "Reading" ability
25 Bang-up
27 Appear on the scene
28 Where Bob Dylan was born: Abbr.
29 Prefix with propyl
30 Kitchen containers

32 "Liza With a Z" Emmy winner
33 Like some income
34 1975 Edward Albee Pulitzer-winning play
35 Takes, as an exam
39 "Vox populi, vox ___"
41 Key of Mozart's "Odense" Symphony
42 Anger
43 Rendezvous
46 Leaders of class struggles?
47 Host Jules of E!
48 Not play subtly
51 Without ___ (dangerously)
53 Jersey wearer, maybe

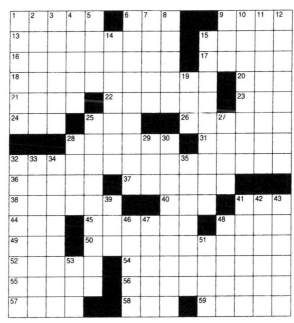

by Brendan Emmett Quigley

ACROSS
1 Alpha particle emitter
7 Admitted guilt for
13 Slips
14 Not for real
16 Fenced-in area
17 Mrs. Lovett's pastries in "Sweeney Todd"
18 Letters at a launch
19 Jelly Roll Morton genre
21 "Gimme ___!"
22 First name in spydom
24 Big wheel at a supermarket?
25 1970's baseball All-Star ___ Colbert
26 "I Still See ___" ("Paint Your Wagon" song)
28 Wall St. market, briefly
29 Broadcast network
30 B team
33 Unattached
34 Jitters
40 Mode of travel pointed in two directions
41 New Testament book: Abbr.
42 Be still, at sea
43 Sticking point?
44 Cornball
46 Organ teacher's field: Abbr.
47 It's tied in back
48 They're made by running water
50 Tognazzi of "La Cage aux Folles"
51 Headphone wearers
53 Tries to get the hard-to-get
55 It may be French or Italian, but not German
56 Latin word usually abbreviated with a single letter
57 Whipper-snapper?
58 Admiral at Guadalcanal, 1943

DOWN
1 A lot of copy shop business
2 Discount oil source
3 Far-reaching
4 Suffix with different
5 Where 1-15 and 1-70 cross
6 Land with a cavalry in Ezekiel
7 Fountain locale
8 Leap for Lipinski
9 Special gift
10 Hesitant question
11 Popular diner
12 Bar offerings
14 Response to a sales clerk
15 Take-charge kind of guy
20 Handy kitchen cooker
23 Currently
25 Home of Literature Nobelist Wole Soyinka
27 Cell part
29 An Adams
31 Currency board abbr.
32 One may get bonded
34 Agreements
35 English novelist Pym
36 Without help
37 Beautiful women
38 Knickknack holder
39 In other words
44 Emote, with "up"
45 "That's disgusting!"
48 Famed sewer
49 Big Apple park
52 "Woe ___" (classic book for "grammarphobes")
54 Natl. League city

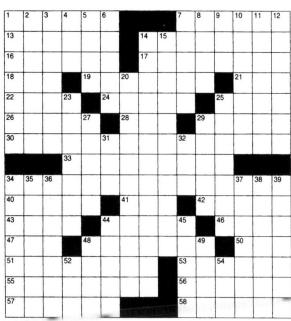

by Manny Nosowsky

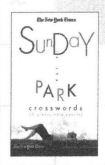

1

```
CORPS  POLL  STOP
OFARC  APIA  HARI
MAYOR  GENTLEMAN
  PATONTHEBACK
STOOPED    VALLI
PETSEMATARY  EEE
ADIEU   UPN
SSS  PITBOSS  MIT
      TOE  USENO
EMT  POTSTARTERS
SOAMI    SPRITES
PUTONEOVERON
INTRANSIT  UGLIS
EDEN  OHOS  NEEDY
SSRS  WALE  DRIER
```

2

```
RABBI  TOTO  PHAT
ELLEN  APEX  AERO
ELAND  KENO  RACY
SARDINECANARD
EYE  REF  NIN  BAA
  TAXISTANDARD
GAIA  TVA  NARNIA
LINT  END   ODER
AMOEBA  TOT  ISLE
SACREDCOWARD
STU  EVA  NBA  TWA
  LATESTBUZZARD
SPAM  RHEE  OHGOD
PETE  SERA  ROUTE
APES  EDIT  SUPER
```

3

```
BICS  EASY  FROZE
ANAT  AREA  LEXUS
SEVERTIES  ATILT
IPANA   TIER  DUE
STL  REMORSELESS
  CRETE   QUO
ESAI  TAIL  PAWED
LADYTENNISSTARS
SPEAR  YEAH  HIRT
  DAM   ROSES
NOTHINGISON  TNT
EMU  POUR  ABBIE
WARES  SKINGRAFT
SHOVE  TELE  ANTE
YAWED  ODED  EDYS
```

4

```
GAFF  RABBI  BOMB
EBRO  EVIAN  OLIO
ALEXTHEORDINARY
RYE  HANSE  MINED
    ZASU   AMT
PETETHEMEDIOCRE
RAINS   APEX  LOX
OTTO  LAYIN  BODE
OER  SAGA   ALTER
FREDTHENOTSOHOT
   OUR   POST
STERN  POISE  APB
KATETHEPASSABLE
IMAM  ORATE  DOIN
DELI  PULED  SUEZ
```

5

```
LABS  RBIS  AMPLY
EDEN  ARNE  QUEUE
AEROSPACE  USERS
FLYWEIGHTTITLE
SELENE   OAF
   TRES  KENYAN
ICK   NUMEROUNO
THEDEADMANSHAND
COPINGSAW   NEE
HOTTER  CRUZ
    REA   SAFARI
 SILVERBRACELET
SIDEA  HEIGHTENS
AGENT  ANTE  CRAM
PHASE  TEES  HOLE
```

6

```
E R R S [ ] A R G U E [ ] A H S O
M E A T [ ] T E E N Y [ ] R O A N
I D L Y [ ] I N T H E H O U S E
T O P M A S T S [ ] S O U R E D [ ]
[ ] H I S S E S [ ] O T S [ ]
M A K E S U R E [ ] R E A L M S
A C I D T E S T [ ] E L L I O T
R A N [ ] Q U A
C R E S T S [ ] S P I T C U R L
Y E R O U T [ ] T I M E L I N E
[ ] A B A [ ] U N S A I D [ ]
S I M P E R [ ] C H O K E D U P
I C E B R E A K E R [ ] N I L E
C O M O [ ] A R O A R [ ] T E N S
K N O X [ ] T A N D Y [ ] S T A T
```

7

```
P O T A T O S A C K R A C E S
I S A T O N E S L E I S U R E
C O N T R O L P I T C H E R S
O L S O N [ ] P O K E S A T
N E H [ ] T O L D O N [ ] S I T E
E M O [ ] E L A I N E S [ ] N A T
T I E O N E O N [ ] S T A [ ]
S O S A D [ ] S E D [ ] A P H I S
[ ] K O S [ ] S E R G E A N T
B O D [ ] N I C E J O B [ ] D A R
I P O D [ ] L A N A T E [ ] A S E
G E N O M E S [ ] E D G E S
S N A P I N S P E C T I O N S
A T T E N T I O N P L E A S E
M O I S T T O W E L E T T E S
```

8

```
♣ C A R [ ] H U S H [ ] O P E N ♥
S O M E [ ] A N K A [ ] C A R O B
O M I T [ ] V E I N [ ] E R I T U
D E C A D E S [ ] O N A T E A R
A R A R A T [ ] P I O N [ ] C T N
[ ] S O I E [ ] S I V A [ ]
M A T C H [ ] M E D I C I N E S
E L O I [ ] J O K E R [ ] C A R A
L I S A B O N E T [ ] F I L E S
[ ] C O I R [ ] R S T U [ ]
N E A [ ] G E L S [ ] O N D E C K
E N N O B L E [ ] R O T U N D A
I T I N A [ ] A R A L [ ] M O R T
L E N I N [ ] R A G E [ ] A L O E
♦ R I N G [ ] Y O U R [ ] S A M ♠
```

9

```
A R T S A L E [ ] I C E B A G
M E A T B A L L [ ] C O O L I E
M A K E L I K E [ ] A S S O R T
O L E R U D [ ] M D L I [ ] C T S
N I C E R [ ] K O O L [ ] A K I M
I T E S [ ] A N N O [ ] L L A M A
A Y N [ ] C L E A R H E A D E D
[ ] T H R E E D M O V I E [ ]
F R E E A N D E A S Y [ ] R D S
L A R R Y [ ] E S T S [ ] M U O N
A P S E [ ] N E T S [ ] R A N T O
T I T [ ] C O P A [ ] R E I N E R
T E A P O T [ ] N O O N T I D E
O R G I E S [ ] D E M E A N O R
P S E U D O [ ] D E S I G N S
```

10

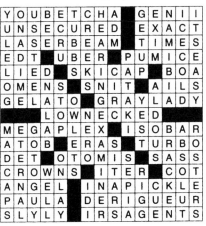

```
Y O U B E T C H A [ ] G E N I I
U N S E C U R E D [ ] E X A C T
L A S E R B E A M [ ] T I M E S
E D T [ ] U B E R [ ] P U M I C E
L I E D [ ] S K I C A P [ ] B O A
O M E N S [ ] S N I T [ ] A I L S
G E L A T O [ ] G R A Y L A D Y
[ ] L O W N E C K E D [ ]
M E G A P L E X [ ] I S O B A R
A T O B [ ] E R A S [ ] T U R B O
D E T [ ] O T O M I S [ ] S A S S
C R O W N S [ ] I T E R [ ] C O T
A N G E L [ ] I N A P I C K L E
P A U L A [ ] D E R I G U E U R
S L Y L Y [ ] I R S A G E N T S
```

11

S	H	A	Q		S	H	I	P	S		G	A	B	S
P	E	R	U		P	E	R	O	T		O	P	A	L
A	N	T	E		A	R	M	O	R		M	E	N	U
		B	A	R	B	A	R	A	B	O	X	E	R	
E	T	H	E	L			E	W	E	R				
J	O	E	C	O	C	K	E	R		D	R	A	M	S
E	R	A		T	A	I	L		D	E	A	D	O	N
C	E	R	F		S	N	I	P	E		H	A	T	E
T	U	T	O	R	S		Z	A	S	U		G	E	E
S	P	Y	R	I		M	A	R	K	S	P	I	T	Z
		S	N	C	C			A	R	O	S	E		
I	T	S	A	D	O	G	S	L	I	F	E			
T	A	C	K		D	R	A	I	N		P	R	A	M
C	L	U	E		A	A	R	O	N		P	O	L	O
H	E	M	S		S	W	A	N	S		Y	E	L	P

12

C	H	E	V	Y		S	H	A	Q		S	P	O	T
A	E	R	I	E		T	O	F	U		T	E	A	R
P	R	I	V	A	T	E	P	R	O	P	E	R	T	Y
O	R	C	A		O	R	S	O		A	P	S	E	S
		L	Y	O	N		A	R	D	E	N	T		
H	I	D	D	E	N	A	G	E	N	D	A			
A	V	A	I	L		A	R	K		D	E	J	A	
W	A	R		P	A	N	G	R	A	M		C	U	B
K	N	E	E		R	O	N		E	P	O	D	E	
		S	E	C	R	E	T	B	A	L	L	O	T	
C	A	R	O	M	S		A	L	D	A				
A	L	I	B	I		Z	U	L	U		T	Y	C	O
C	O	V	E	R	T	O	P	E	R	A	T	I	O	N
T	O	E	S		A	N	O	N		S	E	P	A	L
I	F	S	O		G	E	N	T		P	R	E	X	Y

13

A	N	G	E	S		S	C	R	O	D		C	O	T
D	A	R	I	A		P	I	A	N	O		R	F	K
A	R	E	N	A		O	T	T	E	R		U	F	O
P	R	E	S	B	Y	T	E	R	I	A	N	S		
T	O	N		O	T	R	A		E	A	V	E		
S	W	E	E	T	L	Y		C	R	A	W	D	A	D
		L	O	A		S	E	A	T		E	T	S	
	B	R	I	T	N	E	Y	S	P	E	A	R	S	
P	E	A		A	D	D	S		S	A	C			
J	A	I	A	L	A	I		A	T	M	C	A	R	D
S	U	N	G		F	E	T	A		M	A	I		
	B	E	S	T	I	N	P	R	A	Y	E	R	S	
C	E	O		L	O	C	A	L		D	O	L	E	S
P	A	W		A	R	E	C	A		A	R	I	S	E
A	U	S		T	E	S	T	Y		M	E	A	T	S

14

P	I	E	T	A		B	T	U	S		J	E	L	L
A	S	T	O	R		O	O	N	A		E	R	O	O
I	M	N	O	T	I	N	R	I	G	H	T	N	O	W
R	E	A	L	I	T	Y	T	V		A	S	O	N	E
		A	E	S				A	R	E				
I	L	L	T	R	Y	Y	O	U	L	A	T	E	R	
V	A	L	E		E	N	N	I	S		I	O	N	
A	L	A		B	A	S	A	L	T	S		E	M	O
N	A	M		A	R	N	I	E		S	I	A	M	
	W	A	I	T	F	O	R	T	H	E	T	O	N	E
		F	T	S				O	N	O				
E	X	C	E	L		T	H	I	R	D	R	A	T	E
L	E	A	V	E	Y	O	U	R	N	U	M	B	E	R
I	N	R	E		E	R	G	O		R	E	A	R	S
S	A	A	R		T	E	E	N		E	D	D	I	E

15

C	R	A	G		T	O	J	O		I	N	A	W	E
H	O	R	A		S	T	A	R		C	E	S	A	R
E	A	R	S		K	R	Z	Y	Z	E	W	S	K	I
F	R	O	M	A	T	O	Z		S	C	E	N	E	S
		W	A	R	S		A	G	A	R	S			
S	C	H	I	C	K		G	A	Z	E	T	T	E	S
A	R	E	N	T		M	E	N	S	A		E	D	U
D	O	A	S	I	D	O		G	A	M	B	L	E	D
A	N	D		C	E	R	T	S		S	A	L	M	A
T	E	S	T	C	A	S	E		N	O	R	M	A	N
		H	I	R	E	D		E	D	G	E			
D	E	S	E	R	T		D	I	S	A	R	M	E	D
A	N	T	I	C	H	R	I	S	T		A	O	N	E
S	N	A	R	L		B	E	L	L		P	R	O	P
H	E	S	S	E		I	S	E	E		H	E	L	P

16

```
. H E M A . I B E T . A B U T
T O P O L . D A M E . B O N O
W H I T E R O S E S . O P E L
P O S T P O N E R S . V E A L
. . . S H O T B Y . R E E S E
S C A T . M C A . M A P P E D
H A T . . A L A S K A . . .
1 9 9 4 W O R L D S E R I E S
. . S H R E W D . . C E E
M A S Q U E . A R P . B E L T
A C T U P . S L E E P Y .
S A R A . I N K S L I N G E R
O D O R . M O O S E C A L L S
N I K E . R O U E . A M U S T
S E E D . E T T E . S E G A
```

17

```
R A J . S P E W . S A G A S
S P U R . P O R E . T R A M P
V A L E . A O N E . R A Z O R
P R E F E R R E D S A L A R Y
S T P E T E . . Y O W . .
. . R A K E S . S H I P T O
A T M E . E L L A . A N E A R
T H A N K Y O U L E T T E R S
T R I C E . N E I N . E S S O
N O N E E D . S A T Y R .
. . P I P . R E V S U P
J O B A P P L I C A T I O N S
A R O M A . U N P C . E L B A
M A N I C . S T A T . W A I T
B L A D E . H O S E . R D S
```

18

```
A R C O . D E L F T . N E M O
S A H L . E M I L E . O X E N
S H E L . S O L A R . N I N E
. R E A L I T Y B I T E S .
N A T . I R E . . E T T A S
C H A R L E S T O N C H E W S
O S H E A . U K E . I D L E
. . A C R O B A T I C . .
D I A L . E W E . L A P A Z
A F R I C A N S W A L L O W S
M I T Z I . . H U B . N E A
. D A I L Y D I G E S T S .
L O E B . S A U T E . S O O T
E C C L . A L D E R . T O M E
O T O E . T E E N S . S N E E
```

19

```
I T E M . S P E C . P C L A B
R O S Y . U R S A . R H O N E
A G A R . L E A H . E L U D E
N O U N I F Y I N G M O T I F
. . . A C U E . L E E .
Y A M . A R R A Y E D . S A G
A B O I L . S E A . E L I A
W H O L L Y T H E M E L E S S
L O N E . U K E . N I E L S
S R S . S C O R N E D . K E Y
. . S O C . O N O R . .
J U S T R A N D O M W O R D S
E C L A T . E A S E . B O R E
F L U K E . O N E S . I D E A
F A M E D . N A S H . N E W T
```

20

```
S A F E . S T O O P . L A S E
E D E N . H I N D U . O N C E
A L L D R E S S E D . N Y U K
R A I S E . . G R I L L .
S I X . M O N T O Y A . O P P
. . C O T T O N . B A N T U
R O T O . W H O O P I N G I T
A Z A R I A . . U N S E N T
J O H N N Y J U M P . O R G S
A N I S E . A N T A W N .
S E T . P A Y C A S H . R I P
. H I L T S . . E R I T U
B O A S . W H I C H W A Y I S
U L N A . A B I D E . M A S H
N E S T . N O I S Y . P L A Y
```

21

```
S E A S   W I L D E B E E S T
T A R T   O N E O V E R P A R
U R G E   M E N T A L N O T E
B L O W H A R D S   L E D I N
      P A N T S   A B S E N T
S C R O L L     K N O T
P R E T T Y P E N N Y   C A M
C A N S   A L E   D U P E
A G O   L A D I E S F I R S T
    R E P S   T R A D E S
R A V A G E   F R E O N
E L I T E   D R E A M T E A M
S P R I N G R O L L   H A L O
T H A T D O E S I T   U S E S
S A L E S P I T C H   S E C T
```

22

```
E G O S U R F I N G   S H O D
L A N A T U R N E R   T O R I
P L A Y E D O V E R   D U D S
A L B S   E G A D   E S S E S
S I E N A   S L I C E   E R E
O C T O P I   I N U N I S O N
      E R O D E R   T A U T
M O L O T O V   S T K I T T S
Y V E S   N E S S I E
C U T S H O R T   S T R O D E
O L A   A N T E S   T E X A N
L A L A W   O R C A   D A L I
O T O S   O N I O N R O L L S
G E N T   S E L F D E N I A L
Y S E R   U S E F I N E S S E
```

23

```
T G I F   R I P E   A D A P T
R A N I   E M I L   L O N E R
A T T N   M A S H   T I N N Y
M O O G O O G A I P A N
  S W E R V E   O R G A N S
    R A E   D I P   S W A P
E G R E T   R I G I D   A N A
V O O D O O E C O N O M I C S
A F T   R U D E R   T O T E M
D O O M   T O Y   N C R
E R R A N D   H O O P L A
  Y O O H O O I M H O M E
I D A H O   O B I S   I S I S
T O T E S   W I S E   N E G S
S H A M E   L E T S   E R O O
```

24

```
A U N T   B A S S   Y A W N S
S N E E   A R L O   E T H O S
T R A P   I C E R   S H A R E
H E R E S T H E R E M O T E
M A B E L   T O Y   S S T S
A L Y   A H S   W E B   N U N
    E M B E D   A L E R O
  I L L M O W T H E L A W N
S N A K E   S U R L Y
I S R   R O W   B A A   L B J
R U G S   R O T   S P I R E
  L E T S G O O U T T O E A T
H A S A T   D A R E   P S I S
I T S M E   E D I T   U T N E
S E E P S   N Y S E   P O S T
```

25

```
S A F E   A D H O C   S A G E
C H E X   T I A R A   P U R R
A M A H   E R R O R   I D E A
T E R I Y A K I   D E N I E S
      B E S S   K A R A O K E
R E G I M E   C A M E L
A G A T E   O H N O   B E A
J A P A N E S E I M P O R T S
A D E   L A W N   E L E N A
    A T O M S   B A D R A P
I K E B A N A   S E C T
D I A L O G   P A C H I N K O
L U G E   A N I T A   M I N I
E W E S   T O T E M   E N O L
D A R T   E V A D E   S E X Y
```

26

U	N	N	A	T	U	R	A	L	■	S	A	L	A	D
P	E	A	C	E	P	I	P	E	■	T	R	I	P	E
A	S	S	E	S	S	O	R	S	■	A	N	N	A	L
S	T	A	R	T	■	T	I	S	■	N	I	E	C	E
■	■	■	B	B	Q	■	L	E	A	D	E	N	E	D
T	W	O	■	A	&	E	■	R	&	B	■	■	■	■
H	A	D	A	N	A	I	R	■	M	Y	T	U	R	N
E	V	E	N	■	S	&	L	■	O	R	E	O	■	■
O	Y	S	T	E	R	■	D	I	A	G	O	N	A	L
■	■	B	&	B	■	B	&	O	■	S	L	O	■	■
H	I	G	H	B	R	E	D	■	P	U	P	■	■	■
U	N	L	I	T	■	G	A	T	■	L	A	D	L	E
M	A	O	R	I	■	G	R	A	D	A	T	I	O	N
I	N	B	E	D	■	A	L	L	U	S	I	O	N	S
D	E	E	R	E	■	R	A	C	E	H	O	R	S	E

27

L	O	O	P	T	H	E	L	O	O	P	■	H	O	P
A	N	T	I	H	E	R	O	I	N	E	■	O	P	E
M	E	T	E	O	R	I	T	E	C	R	A	T	E	R
■	■	■	C	R	S	■	■	■	E	L	M	E	R	S
I	B	S	E	N	■	F	I	S	■	E	N	L	A	I
R	I	I	S	■	D	A	M	E	S	■	O	C	T	A
I	L	L	■	M	A	K	E	C	E	R	T	A	I	N
S	L	A	■	A	R	E	A	R	U	G	■	S	O	C
H	I	S	H	O	L	I	N	E	S	S	■	I	N	A
P	O	M	E	■	A	D	I	T	S	■	A	N	A	T
O	N	A	I	R	■	S	T	E	■	I	D	O	L	S
T	A	R	S	A	L	■	■	■	S	W	E	■	■	■
A	I	N	T	G	O	N	N	A	H	A	P	P	E	N
T	R	E	■	E	M	P	I	R	E	S	T	A	T	E
O	E	R	■	D	A	R	K	G	L	A	S	S	E	S

28

G	A	S	B	A	G	S	■	R	O	T	I	F	E	R
Q	U	A	R	L	E	S	■	E	V	A	S	I	V	E
T	R	Y	O	U	T	S	■	S	E	L	E	N	I	C
Y	O	Y	O	M	A	■	L	O	R	I	■	E	D	A
P	R	E	K	I	N	D	E	R	G	A	R	T	E	N
E	A	S	I	N	G	I	N	T	O	■	A	U	N	T
■	■	N	O	R	M	A	S	■	M	I	N	C	E	■
B	I	G	G	U	Y	■	■	T	O	S	E	E	D	■
A	M	E	S	S	■	S	T	R	O	D	E	■	■	■
D	E	N	S	■	H	A	R	D	R	E	S	I	N	S
P	A	D	D	L	E	B	O	A	T	R	A	C	E	S
A	N	A	■	A	L	I	T	■	I	N	H	E	A	T
S	T	R	A	P	I	N	■	A	L	M	A	A	T	A
T	I	M	R	I	C	E	■	C	L	A	N	G	E	R
S	T	E	H	N	O	S	■	S	A	N	D	E	R	S

29

L	O	F	T	S	■	C	A	P	E	■	B	R	A	G
T	U	L	I	P	■	A	L	E	X	■	L	E	T	O
D	R	A	M	A	■	L	O	C	H	■	A	L	O	E
■	■	R	O	C	K	M	U	S	I	C	I	A	N	S
S	T	E	R	E	O	■	■	B	A	R	T	A	B	■
C	O	D	■	S	P	A	S	T	I	C	■	E	L	Y
I	O	U	S	■	■	G	R	O	T	T	O	■	■	■
■	■	P	A	P	E	R	T	R	A	I	L	S	■	■
■	■	D	I	N	E	A	T	■	■	D	O	L	L	■
G	A	P	■	P	R	E	S	E	T	S	■	A	Y	E
O	R	O	M	E	O	■	■	R	A	S	P	E	D	■
S	C	I	S	S	O	R	S	K	I	C	K	S	■	■
S	A	N	D	■	T	O	W	N	■	H	A	T	E	S
I	N	T	O	■	E	L	I	E	■	E	T	A	T	S
P	A	Y	S	■	D	O	M	E	■	T	E	R	S	E

30

A	L	C	O	A	■	A	E	S	O	P	■	G	A	S
J	I	H	A	D	■	D	I	A	N	E	■	O	N	T
O	V	A	T	E	■	E	N	R	O	N	L	O	G	O
B	E	N	■	S	A	L	S	■	N	I	G	E	L	■
■	B	U	M	■	L	E	T	T	S	■	E	L	L	A
T	A	K	E	S	T	H	E	V	A	L	U	E	O	F
R	I	A	T	A	■	I	A	T	E	■	■	■	■	■
A	T	H	O	U	S	A	N	D	I	N	R	O	M	E
■	■	■	R	O	L	F	■	Y	A	H	O	O	■	■
S	Y	M	B	O	L	F	O	R	C	A	R	B	O	N
P	E	E	R	■	D	A	R	E	D	■	A	O	N	■
A	M	N	I	O	■	M	A	S	K	■	T	R	U	■
S	E	T	T	L	E	D	U	P	■	N	O	H	I	T
M	N	O	■	E	X	I	L	E	■	O	B	E	S	E
S	I	R	■	G	O	M	A	D	■	T	I	R	E	S

31

```
R E H A B ■ T O T S ■ T O A D
A V I L A ■ R I O T ■ E N D O
M A T E Y ■ A N T I ■ N E M O
■ ■ C L O C K O F C H A I R
B T U ■ E R E ■ ■ F A U L T S
A E N E A S ■ S P E N T ■ ■
C A L L F O R C O N E ■ F R I
K R I S ■ ■ A O L ■ O R A N
S S T ■ C A R T O F C L O V E
■ ■ B O N E T ■ R A D N E R
S A T U R N ■ C U P ■ T N T
C R O C K O F C A G E S ■ ■
R I N K ■ Y E A R ■ C U R I E
I S E E ■ E T A L ■ O M I T S
P E R T ■ D E N Y ■ D O D O S
```

32

```
B I N G ■ L A P E L ■ A H E M
O D O R ■ A L A M O ■ R A R A
A L W A Y S G O T O O T H E R
S E I N E S ■ ■ K U W A I T
■ ■ D L I I ■ R I T A ■ ■
P E O P L E S F U N E R A L S
I N C A S ■ L I E ■ R E G A L
P E T ■ ■ B E R R A ■ ■ A C U
E R E S T U ■ ■ S I T T E R
O T H E R W I S E T H E Y ■
■ A L L A F L A M E ■ ■
A L I F E ■ R H O ■ A D D T O
W O N T C O M E T O Y O U R S
A W E S O M E ■ H O B N A I L
Y E S ■ M A D ■ S H E ■ L O O
```

33

```
D R A C U L A ■ W A R Z O N E
R O P E S I N ■ A Q U I N A S
A B A S H E D ■ R U B R I C S
B E L T E D ■ O N A ■ C O R E
■ ■ B R O W N S ■ T O N E S
P E D I ■ R O E ■ P E N ■ ■
S T R E A M O F A I R ■ E D O
S C A N D A L O U S R U M O R
T H Y ■ I N F O R M A L I T Y
■ ■ J O T ■ T A O ■ T R E X
F O C U S ■ F E E B L E ■ ■
A V O N ■ B U D ■ E E R I E R
M I L K F E D ■ M A T I L D A
E N T E R E D ■ E C H O I N G
D E S T I N Y ■ W H E R E A S
```

34

```
T R A P ■ M I S S K A N S A S
R E N O ■ A M I T O B L A M E
A S T O ■ S P L I T L E V E L
S C I F I ■ L E T T E R O N E
H O G ■ B R O N C O ■ R I C
T R U E N O R T H ■ B R E T T
V E A L S T E W ■ B R A D Y S
■ ■ M A C S ■ L A I N ■ ■
S O L E U S ■ M A L D E M E R
E C A R D ■ P O P E L E O X I
N O N ■ T E N U R E ■ N O G
S N O W G O O S E ■ S M I T H
I N T H E W R O N G ■ A T I T
N O T O N E I O T A ■ L O C O
G R E A T D A N E S ■ I R A N
```

35

```
A C M E ■ A E R ■ T S E T S E
N O I R ■ J L O ■ O P E R A S
D O N A D A M S ■ R O G E R S
R E D S O X ■ S P A R ■ A D E
E D S E L ■ E I G H T Y S I X
■ ■ S L U R ■ A S Y O U ■ ■
T N T ■ E E N Y ■ ■ G R I T
W O U L D Y O U B E L I E V E
A W R Y ■ ■ M O N A ■ R Y E
■ ■ B R U S H ■ R O S A ■ ■
S H O E P H O N E ■ S N I F F
T A J ■ L A N E ■ S O I R E E
O N E O A R ■ G E T S M A R T
R O T A T E ■ E L O ■ A T M E
M I S T E R ■ V F W ■ L E I S
```

36

```
C U R S   A M B E R   A W A Y
O L E O   W I L M A   F E T A
S C R O L L L O C K   F L O W
M E A N Y   K N E E   A L P S
O R N E R Y   D E R A I L
      S E E S     B R I N E
J E S T   A P A C H E   K E G
O N T   T R I P L E L   E R G
L V I   A N N E A L   O D D S
T Y L E R     M E S H
    L A P S E S   N O M O R E
P A L S   A S A P   I S L A M
E X I T   S Q U A L L L I N E
R I F E   S U N N I   A V O N
U S E R   Y E A S T   W E N D
```

37

```
B R I M S   C A I N   A R G O
R A D I I   A C R E   V E E R
A T E A M   B I O S   A N T E
W I S H I D I D N T K N O W
N O T A   I N S     E T U I S
        M U G S   A G A I N S T
F R U M P     A S P     C E E
L E N   N O W W H A T   E T A
A D D   W E S   D I D O K
T H E W I N D   P E S T
S A R A N   S A G   S O B S
  I D I D N T K N O W T H E N
T R O T   E Y E D   I R A T E
R E N O   A R I A   L U R E R
A D E N   T O N S   D E A L T
```

38

```
M A L I B U   A D D A   F A T
I R O B O T   N O U N   A B O
S T A N Z A   G I S T   T O O
      O H W U T T I H W U T
T E A M S   N I N E   O A T H
U L N A   A B S O R B S
T O O H A T A H W   A P R I L
U P S I D E   A R I A N A
S E E M E   T U O T I T I A W
    A N G I N A L   A S I N
E T C H   A N T S   S L E D S
A W O I A W M U T T O
S I N   L A I N   A N O I N T
E N D   T I N E   M I R R O R
L E O   O N E D   S C R E W Y
```

39

```
S C O W   W H I S K B R O O M
U L N A   H A V E N E E D T O
R E E L   I T A L I A N A R T
G A S K E T   R I F T   Y A H
E N T E R E D   G E N E
  H E R E T I C   D I V A N S
C O P S   I T L L   K A P O K
H U P   D E C E I T S   P S I
I S E R E   H A L O   S L I P
P E D A L S   T A U N T E R
    D U C T   C R E A S E S
I D O   S H I P   I S R A E L
T O M C O L L I N S   T U B A
C L E A R E D O U T   E C O N
H E N N Y P E N N Y   D E B T
```

40

```
H E A D S T A N D S   P I C T
I N D O O R P O O L   A R A W
G O O N T I P T O E   P O R E
H U R T S   R E V E R E N C E
A G E S   L I V E P E R S O N
S H E   S I Z E R   C H I V E
      C I T E R   B E A D E R
C A R O L E D   W R I T E R S
O N A G E R   I H O P S
M O V I N   S W E A T   Y E P
P R E T T Y H A R D   C O D A
L E N A H O R N E   H A D I T
E X I T   G O T A M I N U T E
T I N E   I V E M O V E D O N
E C G S   S E M I D E S E R T
```

41

```
L A P S   L O O S E   H A V E
A R E A   O M A H A   A R A L
S T A N   R E S E T   D E L I
    D E N N I S S I N N E D
O T T   L E S S   S T A T E
D R U M S     C P L   S S S
D A N I E L N A I L E D
S P A N   S A N T A   O S L O
    D W A Y N E Y A W N E D
M P G   E T S     I N A N E
C R A W L   A C I D   G A S
G E R A L D G L A R E D
I V A N   O R O N O   A L F A
L U G E   P I N O N   S O I L
L E E S   E P E E S   H U G E
```

42

```
C U R T I N     R E A D S T O
O P E N B A R   A Y K R O Y D
P I A N I S T   D E C O D E D
S N L   S T E R N O   P A S S
      R E Y   E E N
J A D E S   I S R   C H A S E
U N I S   O D E   W O E F U L
L I V E F R O M N E W Y O R K
E M E E R S   B A T   D O G E
P A R D O   M L B   F A T E S
        H O E   B E Y
R O T C   O R D E A L   N B C
I N E R R O R   T R I B O R O
B E L U S H I   H O N O R E R
S I E S T A S   N E W M A N
```

43

```
L I A R   A M A N A   S T A N
A C R E   L O R E S   T O T E
P E O P L E W I T H T Y P E O
E M U   O R E   Y E L P
L A S T W O R D S   E E R I E
S N E E R   S E E D   D I B S
    A I D   B A R S   Z I P
P E R S O N A L I T I E S
H E Y   E V E S   P U G
A R E A   E X E S   T O G A S
D U C T S   T R E E T R U N K
    A C E S   A V E   R C A
D O N O T W R I T E R I G H T
E N D S   A O L E R   A L O E
F O Y T   M O L D Y   N E R D
```

44

```
S C O T   S L A W   S L O E
P I C A   W A N E   L O T T
A T H I S I S N T R I G H T
Y E S L E T S   S E E Y O U
    F C C   B U D S
B N E I T H E R I S T H I S
L A W N S   P A T   U T E
O S E   S E W   E I G E R
C T R Y T H E N E X T O N E
    E R O S   S T S
E M I L I O   S T R A P I N
D A L L O F T H E A B O V E
I S S O   L I A R   O L E S
T H A W   Y E W S   Y O S T
```

45

```
A T E S T S   C P U   A F A R
T E N P I N   H A N D S O M E
W H E R E A R E Y O U F R O M
A R M Y   P A V E   D O E
R A Y   S T R E P   R I E L
  N O R M   T O S E A   G P A
    F O R M A L   S C E N E I
A U T O M A T E D T E L L E R
A S H T O N   T R O I K A
R T E   M E R C Y   T O N S
E A S T   T I A R A   G U N
  T U E   C M O N   S U M O
T H A T S W H A T I M E A N T
G O T O L D E R   O S A G E S
I T E R   S R O   N U M E R O
```

46

```
F L E M I S H   · L A B E L S
L A Y A N E G G   O N E L A P
I C E S K A T E   K I S S M E
M O L T E N   T W I S T T I E
F R I E D   C S A   E B O N D
L U N D   S H I R T   U N A S
A N E   D A R N G O O D
M A R G A R I T A N O S A L T
    I R I S H M E N   M A H
S L O G   S T E E R   A B R I
I O T A S   E H S   A S I G N
M A I N M E N U   S P L E E N
I D O T O O   N O C H A N C E
L E S I O N   T R A I N C A R
E R E C T S   I N S T E P S
```

47

```
F R A Y   R A I L   R I F T S
Y U L E   E T R E   E M A I L
I T S A   C L A N   F A N N Y
  H O R S E A N D B U G G Y
    N O D S   L E E
G I S   R E T R I A L   A S A
A D M I T   I D S   P L U S
M E A T A N D P O T A T O E S
M A L T   O N E   M A U D E
A L L   G R A N I T E   D E T
    S O S   G O N G
  N I C K E L A N D D I M E
C O B R A   A R O D   V I S E
A D E E R   C A R L   E S P Y
N E T W T   E P E E   N O N E
```

48

```
E R I N   S R T A S   N A M E
S O S A   C O A C H   E V A N
Q U I T D A Y D R E A M I N G
S E N H O R A S   L E V E R
    A G A L   M O M S
  D O N T B E S O N A I V E
M E N S A   E V E   S E V E
E L I   G E T R E A L   X E R
A V O N   G A T   I S E R E
  E N O U G H A L R E A D Y
    U S S R   A I N T
S L A V E   S O B E R E S T
C O M E D O W N T O E A R T H
A L I A   W E I S S   P L E A
B L E U   E S T E E   S E M I
```

49

```
L I M B   A T O D D S   O S S
O N E A   C O H E R E   D E W
B A L C O N Y S E A T   I L E
  S T O V E   P B S   O L D
A L O N E   T I L   J U T E
H U R   R A I N Y S E A S O N
A M M O   R E V   H A P
  P E N N Y S E R E N A D E
    E R A   R U R   N A V E
C O M P A N Y S E A L   T A X
S C A M   E E R   I N A P T
H U D   A B A   A D O B E
A L E   M A R K E T S H A R E
R A D   E L N I N O   I S O N
P R O   R E S T O N   T E N T
```

50

```
D O T S   C A T S   B A M B I
O R A N   O R E O   A H E A D
R A M A   N E R F   L O N G S
S C I F I F A N T A S Y
A L L U D E S   M I A M I A N
Y E S S I R   S U M   A S H E
    D E E P S   A T B A T
  H I F I E Q U I P M E N T
P A W A T   U N C L E
E R I C   O A K   A B U T O N
G E N E R A L   B Y A N O S E
  W I F I H O T S P O T S
L A K E S   Z U N I   I B E T
B R I S K   E L E M   L A N E
J E T T Y   R A R E   E D D A
```

51

P	A	L	O	O	K	A	■	■	M	I	C	A	H
S	T	A	N	D	O	F	F	■	T	O	B	A	G	O
A	N	T	E	D	A	T	E	■	R	O	M	M	E	L
L	O	I	N	S	■	E	A	M	O	N	■	E	L	Y
M	O	N	O	■	A	R	S	O	N	■	T	R	I	M
S	N	O	■	T	R	Y	T	O	■	A	R	O	M	A
■	■	M	E	T	O	O	■	S	H	O	O	I	N	
■	P	R	E	S	S	U	R	E	P	O	I	N	T	
S	H	A	N	T	Y	■	F	A	I	L	S	■	■	
T	O	P	S	Y	■	C	A	S	E	D	■	H	U	M
I	T	S	A	■	P	O	M	E	S	■	S	E	P	T
P	O	T	■	S	O	L	I	D	■	T	H	E	R	E
P	L	A	T	T	E	■	N	O	T	S	O	H	O	T
L	A	R	I	A	T	■	E	U	R	O	P	E	A	N
E	B	S	E	N	■	■	■	T	E	S	S	E	R	A

52

S	T	E	A	D	I	C	A	M	■	E	X	P	E	L
W	I	N	N	E	B	A	G	O	■	A	M	U	S	E
I	N	N	K	E	E	P	E	R	■	T	A	M	P	A
S	C	U	L	P	T	■	L	E	S	A	S	P	I	N
S	T	I	E	S	■	D	O	N	A	T	■	S	O	N
■	■	■	I	V	A	N	O	V	■	D	I	N	E	
■	C	O	A	X	I	N	G	■	O	P	E	R	A	S
S	I	N	C	E	R	E	■	P	R	O	L	O	G	S
A	G	E	N	D	A	■	B	E	E	L	I	N	E	
W	A	R	E	■	G	L	E	N	D	A	■	■	■	
E	R	E	■	W	O	O	D	S	■	R	E	M	A	P
D	I	E	R	E	S	I	S	■	V	I	R	I	L	E
O	L	L	I	E	■	T	I	M	E	Z	O	N	E	S
F	L	E	C	K	■	E	D	I	T	E	D	O	U	T
F	O	R	K	S	■	R	E	A	S	S	E	R	T	S

53

C	L	U	B	■	S	H	E	L	F	■	E	L	K	S
L	I	N	E	■	H	O	M	E	R	■	L	E	A	K
E	L	I	E	■	A	L	I	V	E	■	F	A	Z	E
F	I	T	T	O	B	E	T	I	E	D	■	S	O	W
■	■	R	U	B	S	■	■	P	A	T	H	O	S	
C	H	E	E	R	Y	■	E	R	A	S	E	■	■	
H	O	L	D	S	■	C	R	A	S	H	D	I	E	T
E	P	A	■	D	O	W	N	S	■	H	A	H		
F	I	N	A	L	E	D	I	T	■	A	B	O	V	E
■	■	L	I	N	E	N	■	U	S	O	P	E	N	
T	H	R	I	F	T	■	O	S	H	A	■	■	■	
A	A	A	■	T	U	R	N	T	H	E	T	I	D	E
G	I	Z	A	■	R	O	U	T	E	■	M	A	I	D
U	K	E	S	■	E	L	D	E	R	■	A	G	E	D
P	U	S	H	■	S	E	E	R	S	■	N	O	S	Y

54

S	A	T	■	K	R	I	L	L	■	T	I	L	T	S
P	E	R	■	I	N	D	I	A	■	I	C	A	H	N
I	R	E	■	L	A	S	T	S	A	M	U	R	A	I
E	I	E	I	O	■	■	H	E	R	B	■	A	N	T
L	E	S	T	W	E	F	O	R	G	E	T	■	■	
■	■	■	S	A	B	E	■	■	O	R	A	N	G	E
C	H	A	■	T	R	A	I	T	■	■	C	O	E	D
L	I	S	T	T	O	S	T	A	R	B	O	A	R	D
A	R	I	A	■	■	T	O	N	E	R	■	H	E	Y
D	E	S	I	R	E	■	■	T	A	U	S	■	■	
■	■	■	L	O	S	T	H	E	R	S	H	E	E	P
S	T	A	■	O	S	H	A	■	■	S	A	R	G	E
L	U	S	T	F	O	R	L	I	F	E	■	O	R	E
A	B	A	S	E	■	E	A	S	E	L	■	D	E	L
P	A	P	E	R	■	E	S	T	E	S	■	E	T	S

55

N	A	P	A	■	A	P	S	E	S	■	■	O	F	F
I	C	E	S	■	B	O	O	N	S	■	A	P	I	E
C	H	E	S	T	S	O	F	D	R	A	W	E	R	S
E	E	L	■	H	O	R	A	S	■	F	A	C	E	T
■	■	■	T	A	R	■	■	A	O	L	■	■	■	
L	I	G	H	T	B	U	L	B	J	O	K	E	■	
I	D	L	E	S	■	R	U	R	A	L	■	F	R	O
S	E	E	M	■	S	I	L	E	X	■	B	R	A	M
T	E	A	■	S	E	A	L	S	■	S	I	E	G	E
■	■	M	A	T	C	H	S	T	I	C	K	M	E	N
■	■	G	A	T	■	■	G	R	E	■	■	■		
S	C	A	N	T	■	D	R	A	N	O	■	U	S	A
T	H	R	E	E	P	R	E	S	I	D	E	N	T	S
E	A	T	S	■	S	A	D	A	T	■	R	I	O	T
M	R	S	■	■	S	T	O	N	E	■	E	X	P	O

56

```
U R A L  ■ S A N E ■ S C U M
G E N[EVA]■ I T H O T ■ O H N O
A M I R ■ S I E R R A N[EVA]D A
N O M ■ F L E A ■ E M I L E ■
D U A N E E D D Y ■ P A I R S
A N T O N Y ■ ■ O W S ■ E G O
■ T E E D ■ M I K E ■ T R O Y
■ ■ L I T T L E E V A ■ ■
B I B S ■ W I L L ■ A S I F
A M O ■ D A D ■ C L E R I C
S P U M E ■ A T T H E R E A R
■ A L I C E ■ R O O T ■ S N[EVA]
E L[EVA]T O R C A R S ■ P I C S
P E R T ■ A R I S E ■ A G E S
A D D S ■ S O L O ■ K N E E
```

57

```
J A M A I C A ■ N A C H O S
O N A T E A R ■ D E F L E C T
C O N T O R T ■ R E L A X E R
K I D ■ H E F T E D ■ S A L E
■ N A Y ■ O O H S ■ M S D O S
O T T O ■ F R E S C O I S T S
S E E Y A ■ M A Y O R S ■ ■
A D D O N S ■ B A S A L T
■ D E I C E R ■ L U C I E
D E L I N E A T E S ■ E R M A
I L I E D ■ P U G H ■ S O O ■
M A L T ■ M O I R E S ■ S R A
S P I E D O N ■ E L A S T I C
U S E R I D S ■ T V G U I D E
M E S S E S ■ S E A N C E S
```

58

```
A W E D ■ S E C O N D R A T E
C H A T ■ I W A S F R A M E D
T A S S ■ T I M E L I M I T S
S T Y ■ P I N E ■ ■ A C R E
N A G G I N G ■ C O R D I A L
A D O P T S ■ M A R I A ■
I R I S H ■ B O B C O S T A S
V A N ■ S I D E A ■ W I E
E G G B E A T E R ■ A G O R A
■ A N G E L ■ S T O P G O
S T I N G E R ■ S H I P O U T
P E N D ■ ■ G I R T ■ T I T
A N T I C I P A T E ■ L A T E
N E W T O N S L A W ■ I T A R
S T O O D G U A R D ■ T O R S
```

59

```
H A N G ■ E P S O M ■ I H O P
O N E A ■ P O P P A ■ G U L L
S T A R ■ I C E I N ■ U R G E
S I T B A C K A N D R E L A X
■ ■ L P S ■ K E Y E S ■ ■
M I M E O ■ P O D ■ L S A T S
E W E ■ R E F ■ M I S C U E
D O W N F O R T H E C O U N T
I N L A I D ■ H A G ■ R E A
A T S I X ■ R E D ■ B L A S T
■ ■ L I M E D ■ O O O ■ ■
C O M E T O T E R M S W I T H
A X E D ■ L I V E N ■ E D A M
S E M I ■ T R I N I ■ N I N O
K N O T ■ S E L E S ■ D O G S
```

60

```
L E N O ■ D F L A T ■ A S T I
E V I L ■ A R O M A ■ M E I R
S A G E ■ M E T E R ■ B R A E
■ H O U S E T R A I L E R S
A C T ■ R E O ■ ■ M E N A T
F A C I A L F E A T U R E S ■
A T A L L ■ R U B S ■ ■
R O P E ■ P A R K S ■ A T R A
■ E A S E ■ S T R E P
■ C A R T R I D G E C L I P S
T R E A T ■ ■ O V A ■ E S O
B E R M U D A S H O R T S ■
S W A M ■ E B O O K ■ O O P S
P E T E ■ F L U M E ■ G U R U
S L E D ■ T Y P E D ■ A T O P
```

61

A	R	I	S	E		R	A	B	B	I		B	A	T
L	U	N	A	R		A	L	L	A	N		A	R	E
V	E	I	L	O	F	T	I	E	R	S		B	E	E
A	S	T	U	T	E		T	A	R		R	Y	A	N
			D	I	V	A		T	I	N	E	S		
A	L	S		C	E	N	T	S	O	F	S	I	T	E
L	A	M	S		R	N	A			L	I	T	E	R
G	N	A	T		S	A	U	N	A		S	T	A	N
E	A	T	E	N		P	A	N		T	E	S	S	
R	I	T	E	O	F	W	E	I	G	H		R	E	T
		E	R	R	O	R		L	E	E	R			
M	A	R	S		R	E	A		L	I	A	B	L	E
U	R	I		P	E	A	C	E	O	F	M	E	E	T
T	I	N		A	S	T	H	E		E	I	E	I	O
T	A	G		O	T	H	E	R		R	E	R	A	N

62

C	A	P		M	U	O	N	S		C	H	A	R
A	P	U		M	E	N	T	A	L	I	M	A	G	E
R	O	B		R	U	B	B	E	R	N	O	S	E	S
E	L	L		I	S	A		S	E	N	A	T	E	
E	L	I		S	E	R	F	S			G	E	E	
R	O	C	A			A	I	R		B	O	N	D	
E	X	T	R	A	B	A	T	T	E	R	Y			
D	I	V	I	D	E	D	C	A	P	I	T	A	L	S
		D	E	N	V	E	R	O	M	E	L	E	T	
I	N	R	E		T	I	L			S	T	A	R	
S	I	E		L	L	A	M	A		E	V	A		
I	N	C	A	S	H		L	E	I		R	E	D	
T	E	A	M	M	A	N	A	G	E	R		E	N	D
M	A	S	C	A	R	A	C	A	S	E		G	E	L
E	M	T	S		E	M	C	E	E			O	D	E

63

N	A	M	E	N	A	M	E	S		E	A	R	L	S
I	N	A	C	I	R	C	L	E		A	R	E	A	S
P	U	T	O	N	E	S	F	O	O	T	I	N	I	T
S	T	E	L	E			U	N	I	S	O	N	S	
			I	T	A		P	L	A	N	T			
O	R	R		O	I	S	E			O	S	S	A	
P	O	I	S	O	N	P	E	N	L	E	T	T	E	R
A	D	V	E	N	T	U	R	E	I	S	L	A	N	D
L	E	A	V	E	I	N	S	U	S	P	E	N	S	E
S	O	L	E			A	F	A	R		K	E	N	
			R	A	B	A	T		S	E	W			
A	P	P	A	R	A	T			S	A	N	T	A	
G	A	I	N	E	D	A	D	M	I	S	S	I	O	N
E	L	E	C	T		L	E	S	S	O	N	T	W	O
S	P	R	E	E		L	A	S	T	S	T	A	N	D

64

S	P	I	T	C	U	R	L		C	A	N	V	A	S
P	I	N	H	O	L	E	S		A	N	O	I	N	T
R	E	D	E	M	A	N	D		K	O	T	T	E	R
E	P	I	C	E	N	E		P	E	T	N	A	M	E
E	A	R	L	S			R	A	S	H	O	M	O	N
			N	A	U	T	I	C	A	L		E	W	I	N	G
				B	O	B	B	Y	O	R	R		N	E	T
D	O	H			A	R	O	M	A			A	S	H
U	N	O		T	R	A	V	A	N	T	I			
M	E	T	E	R		D	A	R	K	A	G	E	S
P	O	P	M	U	S	I	C			I	N	C	A	N
S	N	A	P	S	T	O		L	A	L	O	L	L	O
T	O	N	I	T	E		L	I	V	E	B	A	I	T
E	N	T	R	E	E		O	P	E	N	L	I	N	E
R	E	S	E	E	D		B	O	R	D	E	R	E	D

65

S	P	A	T		S	A	I	L		M	I	R	E	D
I	O	T	A		E	B	R	O		Y	O	U	R	E
N	U	T	C	R	A	C	K	E	R	S	U	I	T	E
A	N	Y	H	O	W		S	W	A	T		N	E	D
I	D	S		W	A	C		S	P	I	T			
			A	S	T	R	O		S	Q	U	A	T	S
A	M	A	T		E	E	L	S		U	R	I	A	H
B	O	L	T	F	R	O	M	T	H	E	B	L	U	E
R	A	T	I	O		N	O	R	A		A	S	T	A
A	T	O	L	L	S		S	A	T	I	N			
			A	L	A	S		Y	R	S		A	C	C
A	S	A		O	A	T	S		A	N	I	M	A	L
S	C	R	E	W	B	A	L	L	C	O	M	E	D	Y
P	A	N	A	M		R	O	O	K		A	B	E	D
S	N	O	R	E		E	G	O	S		M	A	T	E

66

S	U	M	A	C	S		C	B	S		S	T	A	T
A	T	O	N	A	L		O	L	E		L	E	A	R
W	I	N	D	T	U	N	N	E	L		E	S	A	U
I	C	E	R		S	E	A	N		S	E	T		
N	A	T	E		H	A	N	D	P	U	P	P	E	T
		T	R	Y				U	P	S	I	Z	E	
A	G	A	T	E		G	R	A	S	P		L	I	N
F	I	N	I	S	H	I	N	G	S	E	C	O	N	D
R	A	T		P	A	S	S	E		R	O	T	E	S
O	N	E	T	O	N				E	S	P			
S	T	R	I	N	G	B	E	A	N		A	D	A	M
		O	D	D		L	A	R	D		P	E	L	E
B	L	O	B		B	E	S	T	S	E	L	L	E	R
M	I	M	I		R	A	Y		U	S	E	F	U	L
W	E	S	T		A	K	A		P	L	A	T	T	E

67

J	I	V	E		A	S	A	B	C		W	I	T	S
O	T	O	E		L	O	Y	A	L		O	R	A	N
C	O	U	N	T	B	A	S	I	E		O	I	S	E
K	O	S		R	U	R		L	A	R	D	N	E	R
			C	O	M		B	O	N	E	Y	A	R	D
A	T	B	A	T		H	I	R	S	C	H			
G	A	R	B		T	U	G		E	D	E	R	L	E
O	T	I	C		U	N	B	A	R		R	O	A	D
B	A	T	A	A	N		A	R	S		M	A	N	Y
			L	E	A	R	N	T		D	A	N	E	S
S	L	A	L	O	M	E	D		M	E	N			
W	A	G	O	N	E	R		L	I	P		T	A	J
I	S	A	W		L	O	U	I	S	P	R	I	M	A
N	E	V	A		T	O	G	A	S		I	N	E	Z
G	R	E	Y		S	T	O	R	M		B	E	N	Z

68

F	L	O	O	D	H₂O	G	A	T	E		S	E	A	H₂O
I	R	A	N	I		M	O	O	R		C	L	E	W
R	O	S	E	S		A	N	N	E	M	E	A	R	A
E	N	T	R	A	N	C	E	S		A	N	N	O	Y
H₂O			E	R	A			F	Y	I				
W	A	T	E	R	W	A	T	E	R		C	H	E	W
O	C	A	L	A		B	A	S	E		S	A	S	H
R	U	M		Y	A	C	H	T	E	D		S	K	I
K	R	I	S		S	T	O	A		O	C	T	E	T
S	A	L	A		E	V	E	R	Y	W	H	E	R	E
			M	U	S			A	N	E				H₂O
H	O	M	E	R		P	A	C	H	E	L	B	E	L
O	N	I	O	N	R	O	L	L		A	S	A	M	I
T	E	L	L		A	R	G	O		S	E	R	I	N
H₂O	B	E	D		H	E	A	D	H₂O	T	A	B	L	E

69

S	C	O	O	P		E	R	N		S	C	H	M	O
C	O	N	G	A		T	A	O		C	L	A	R	K
A	D	I	E	U		H	O	T	S	H	O	W	E	R
B	E	T	E	L	G	E	U	S	E		U	S	D	A
			S	C	A	L	L	O	P	E	D			
E	S	E		E	L	S		B	A	L	I	H	A	I
X	P	R	I	Z	E		G	A	L	L	E	O	N	S
I	R	I	N	A		H	A	D		I	S	O	N	E
L	I	C	E	N	S	E	D		E	S	T	H	E	R
E	T	H	A	N	O	L		S	U	I		A	X	E
			R	E	I	M	B	U	R	S	E			
E	T	O	N		L	E	O	T	O	L	S	T	O	Y
S	U	P	E	R	S	T	A	R		A	S	I	D	E
O	B	E	S	E		E	R	A		N	I	K	E	S
S	A	N	T	O		D	D	S		D	E	I	S	M

70

D	U	C		W	A	F	T		E	F	F	U	S	E
O	N	O		I	C	E	R		X	R	A	T	E	D
I	Z	V	E	S	T	I	A		T	U	N	N	E	Y
T	I	E	S		I	G	N		R	I	C	E	R	S
	P	R	O	P	I	N	Q	U	I	T	Y			
			S	B	A		S	U	N	N	Y		F	R	I
I	N	T	E	N	T		I	I	S		A	L	A	N
R	O	O	S	E	V	E	L	T	I	S	L	A	N	D
K	A	R	O		S	K	I		C	H	A	T	T	Y
S	H	Y		S	T	E	T	S		E	M	S		
			R	E	A	D	Y	T	O	R	O	C	K	
P	T	B	O	A	T		B	A	D		D	R	N	O
I	O	L	A	N	I		A	S	I	S	E	E	I	T
C	R	I	S	C	O		S	I	S	I		E	F	T
T	O	P	T	E	N		E	S	T	D		N	E	O

71

A	G	O	G	■	U	P	S	E	T	■	N	E	W	T
L	O	B	E	■	G	O	T	T	I	■	I	S	E	E
P	R	O	A	T	H	L	E	T	E	■	G	A	P	E
O	P	E	R	A	■	S	M	A	S	H	H	I	T	S
■	■	U	R	L	■	■	■	O	U	T	■	■	■	■
■	S	U	P	P	O	R	T	I	N	G	C	A	S	T
S	H	H	■	S	C	O	R	N	■	S	A	N	T	A
A	A	H	S	■	H	O	U	N	D	■	P	I	E	D
A	M	U	C	K	■	S	T	I	E	S	■	S	E	A
B	E	H	I	N	D	T	H	E	W	H	E	E	L	■
■	■	■	S	I	R	■	■	■	Y	O	N	■	■	■
C	A	B	S	T	A	N	D	S	■	V	A	L	U	E
O	S	L	O	■	F	O	R	T	H	E	B	E	S	T
S	T	I	R	■	T	O	N	E	R	■	L	E	N	A
T	O	P	S	■	S	N	O	W	S	■	E	R	A	S

72

F	L	O	■	L	E	A	R	■	R	E	D	C	A	P
L	O	U	■	O	R	N	E	■	I	N	A	R	U	T
O	C	T	■	C	L	E	F	■	N	O	M	A	D	S
P	A	P	A	H	E	M	I	N	G	W	A	Y	■	■
P	L	U	M	S	■	I	L	E	■	■	T	O	F	U
Y	E	T	I	■	M	A	M	A	L	E	O	N	E	S
■	■	S	T	A	■	S	T	A	N	■	E	T	E	■
B	A	S	S	I	S	T	■	O	N	O	R	D	E	R
O	H	O	■	P	O	O	H	■	E	S	O	■	■	■
B	A	B	Y	S	N	O	O	K	S	■	G	U	S	T
O	S	S	A	■	T	R	E	■	O	U	N	C	E	■
■	■	T	H	E	T	H	R	E	E	B	E	A	R	S
S	H	O	O	T	S	■	O	N	M	E	■	B	E	T
A	U	R	O	R	A	■	R	E	M	Y	■	L	E	E
G	E	Y	S	E	R	■	S	R	A	S	■	E	N	D

73

I	M	A	G	E	■	E	T	N	A	■	P	A	P	A
R	A	N	O	N	■	A	G	I	N	■	A	B	E	T
A	C	C	O	U	N	T	I	N	G	■	R	U	S	T
■	■	D	R	U	■	F	O	R	T	A	S	T	E	■
S	A	L	I	E	N	T	■	Y	O	D	E	L	S	■
S	P	U	D	S	■	H	A	T	■	R	E	S	E	T
S	O	L	E	■	B	A	N	A	N	A	■	■	■	■
■	P	L	A	C	E	L	I	K	E	H	O	M	E	■
■	■	R	A	I	S	E	D	■	N	E	M	O	■	■
A	M	U	S	E	■	A	E	R	■	S	T	R	I	P
S	A	T	E	E	N	■	S	O	T	H	E	R	E	■
T	I	M	E	L	I	K	E	■	A	R	E	■	■	■
E	T	O	N	■	T	H	E	P	R	E	S	E	N	T
R	A	S	A	■	R	A	N	I	■	A	L	C	O	A
N	I	T	S	■	O	N	Y	X	■	K	Y	O	T	O

74

P	L	A	S	M	■	H	A	G	■	■	G	I	R	D
R	A	T	I	O	N	A	L	E	■	P	A	T	H	O
I	R	O	N	S	I	D	E	S	■	E	P	S	O	N
C	O	A	C	H	C	A	R	T	E	R	■	A	D	E
E	S	S	E	■	O	B	S	E	S	S	■	L	E	D
D	A	T	■	W	I	L	■	P	E	R	U	S	E	■
■	■	M	O	S	A	I	C	■	C	I	L	I	A	■
B	U	S	I	N	E	S	S	A	S	U	S	U	A	L
O	N	E	N	D	■	T	O	N	I	T	E	■	■	■
B	E	A	N	E	D	■	I	T	E	■	A	R	T	■
F	A	S	■	R	E	P	A	S	S	■	E	M	I	R
O	R	C	■	F	I	R	S	T	F	A	M	I	L	Y
S	N	A	F	U	■	O	N	E	O	N	O	N	E	S
S	E	P	A	L	■	F	E	R	R	E	T	O	U	T
E	D	E	N	■	S	R	S	■	T	E	R	P	S	■

75

R	A	D	I	U	M	■	■	P	L	E	D	T	O
E	R	R	A	T	A	■	I	L	L	U	S	O	R	Y
S	T	A	L	A	G	■	M	E	A	T	P	I	E	S
U	S	S	■	H	O	T	J	A	Z	Z	■	D	A	T
M	A	T	A	■	G	O	U	D	A	■	N	A	T	E
E	L	I	S	A	■	A	S	E	■	A	I	R	E	R
S	E	C	O	N	D	S	T	R	I	N	G	E	R	S
■	■	F	O	O	T	L	O	O	S	E	■	■	■	■
A	B	U	N	D	L	E	O	F	N	E	R	V	E	S
C	A	N	O	E	■	R	O	M	■	L	I	E	T	O
C	R	A	W	■	H	O	K	E	Y	■	A	N	A	T
O	B	I	■	R	A	V	I	N	E	S	■	U	O	S
R	A	D	I	U	M	E	N	■	C	H	A	S	E	S
D	R	E	S	S	I	N	G	■	C	E	T	E	R	A
S	A	D	I	S	T	■	■	H	A	L	S	E	Y	■

The New York Times

Crossword Puzzles

The #1 name in crosswords

Available at your local bookstore or online at nytimes.com/nytstore

Coming Soon!

Will Shortz Presents Fun in the Sun Crossword Puzzles Omnibus	0-312-37041-5	$11.95/$14.95 Can.
How to Conquer The New York Times Crossword Puzzle	0-312-36554-3	$9.95/$11.95 Can.
Afternoon Delight Crosswords	0-312-37071-7	$6.95/$8.50 Can.
Favorite Day Crosswords: Tuesday	0-312-37072-5	$6.95/$8.50 Can.
Crosswords for a Mental Edge	0-312-37069-5	$6.95/$8.50 Can.

Special Editions

Brainbuilder Crosswords	0-312-35276-X	$6.95/$8.50 Can.
Fitness for the Mind Crosswords Vol. 2	0-312-35278-6	$10.95/$13.50 Can.
Vocabulary Power Crosswords	0-312-35199-2	$10.95/$13.50 Can.
Will Shortz Xtreme Xwords Puzzles	0-312-35203-4	$6.95/$8.50 Can.
Will Shortz's Greatest Hits	0-312-34242-X	$8.95/$10.95 Can.
Super Sunday Crosswords	0-312-33115-0	$10.95/$13.50 Can.
Will Shortz's Funniest Crosswords Vol. 2	0-312-33960-7	$9.95/$11.95 Can.
Will Shortz's Funniest Crosswords	0-312-32489-8	$9.95/$11.95 Can.
Will Shortz's Sunday Favorites	0-312-32488-X	$9.95/$11.95 Can.
Crosswords for a Brain Workout	0-312-32610-6	$6.95/$8.50 Can.
Crosswords to Boost Your Brainpower	0-312-32033-7	$6.95/$8.50 Can.
Crossword All-Stars	0-312-31004-8	$9.95/$11.95 Can.
Will Shortz's Favorites	0-312-30613-X	$9.95/$11.95 Can.
Ultimate Omnibus	0-312-31622-4	$17.95/$21.95 Can.

Daily Crosswords

Daily Crossword Puzzles Vol. 72	0-312-35260-3	$9.95/$11.95 Can.
Fitness for the Mind Vol. 1	0-312-34955-6	$10.95/$13.50 Can.
Crosswords for the Weekend	0-312-34332-9	$9.95/$11.95 Can.
Monday through Friday Vol. 2	0-312-31459-0	$9.95/$11.95 Can.
Monday through Friday	0-312-30058-1	$9.95/$11.95 Can.
Daily Crosswords Vol. 71	0-312-34858-4	$9.95/$11.95 Can.
Daily Crosswords Vol. 70	0-312-34239-X	$9.95/$11.95 Can.

Volumes 57-69 also available

Easy Crosswords

Easy Crossword Puzzles Vol. 7	0-312-35261-1	$9.95/$11.95 Can.
Easy Crosswords Vol. 6	0-312-33957-7	$10.95/$13.50 Can.
Easy Crosswords Vol. 5	0-312-32438-3	$9.95/$11.95 Can.

Volumes 2-4 also available

Tough Crosswords

Tough Crosswords Vol. 13	0-312-34240-3	$10.95/$13.50 Can.
Tough Crosswords Vol. 12	0-312-32442-1	$10.95/$13.50 Can.
Tough Crosswords Vol. 11	0-312-31456-6	$10.95/$13.50 Can.

Volumes 9-10 also available

Sunday Crosswords

Sunday Brunch Crossword Puzzles	0-312-36557-8	$6.95/$8.50
Everyday Sunday	0-312-36106-8	$6.95/$8.50 Can.
Sunday Puzzle Omnibus Vol. 32	0-312-36066-5	$9.95/$11.95 Can.
Sunday Morning Crossword Puzzles	0-312-35672-2	$6.95/$8.50 Can.
Sunday in the Park Crosswords	0-312-35197-6	$6.95/$8.50 Can.
Sunday Crosswords Vol. 30	0-312-33538-5	$9.95/$11.95 Can.
Sunday Crosswords Vol. 29	0-312-32038-8	$9.95/$11.95 Can.

Large-Print Crosswords

Large-Print Crosswords for Your Bedside	0-312-34245-4	$10.95/$13.50 Can.
Large-Print Will Shortz's Favorite Crosswords	0-312-33959-3	$10.95/$13.50 Can.
Large-Print Big Book of Easy Crosswords	0-312-33958-5	$12.95/$15.95 Can.
Large-Print Big Book of Holiday Crosswords	0-312-33092-8	$12.95/$15.95 Can.
Large-Print Crosswords for Your Coffeebreak	0-312-33109-6	$10.95/$13.50 Can.
Large-Print Crosswords for a Brain Workout	0-312-32612-2	$10.95/$13.50 Can.
Large Print Crosswords to Boost Your Brainpower	0-312-32037-X	$11.95/$14.95 Can.
Large-Print Easy Omnibus	0-312-32439-1	$12.95/$15.95 Can.
Large-Print Daily Crosswords Vol. 2	0-312-33111-8	$10.95/$13.50 Can.
Large-Print Daily Crosswords	0-312-31457-4	$10.95/$13.50 Can.
Large-Print Omnibus Vol. 6	0-312-34861-4	$12.95/$15.95 Can.
Large-Print Omnibus Vol. 5	0-312-32036-1	$12.95/$15.95 Can.

Previous volumes also available

Omnibus

Crosswords for a Long Weekend	0-312-36560-8	$11.95/$14.95 Can.
Crosswords for a Relaxing Vacation	0-312-36696-7	$11.95/$14.95 Can.
Holiday Cheer Crossword Puzzles	0-312-36126-2	$11.95/$14.95 Can.
Supersized Sunday Crosswords	0-312-36122-X	$16.95/$22.95 Can.
Biggest Beach Crossword Omnibus	0-312-35667-6	$11.95/$14.95 Can.
Weekend Away Crossword Puzzle Omnibus	0-312-35669-2	$11.95/$14.95 Can.
Weekend at Home Crossword Puzzle Omnibus	0-312-35670-6	$11.95/$14.95 Can.
Sunday Crossword Omnibus Volume 9	0-312-35666-8	$11.95/$14.95 Can.
Lazy Sunday Crossword Puzzle Omnibus	0-312-35279-4	$11.95/$14.95 Can.
Supersized Book of Easy Crosswords	0-312-35277-8	$14.95/$21.95 Can.
Crosswords for a Weekend Getaway	0-312-35198-4	$11.95/$14.95 Can.
Crossword Challenge	0-312-33951-8	$11.95/$15.95 Can.
Giant Book of Holiday Crosswords	0-312-34927-0	$11.95/$14.95 Can.
Big Book of Holiday Crosswords	0-312-33533-4	$11.95/$14.95 Can.
Tough Omnibus Vol. 1	0-312-32441-3	$11.95/$14.95 Can.
Easy Omnibus Vol. 5	0-312-36123-8	$11.95/$14.95 Can.
Easy Omnibus Vol. 4	0-312-34859-2	$11.95/$14.95 Can.
Easy Omnibus Vol. 3	0-312-33537-7	$11.95/$14.95 Can.
Easy Omnibus Vol. 2	0-312-32035-3	$11.95/$14.95 Can.
Daily Omnibus Vol. 16	0-312-36104-1	$11.95/$14.95 Can.
Daily Omnibus Vol. 15	0-312-34856-8	$11.95/$14.95 Can.
Daily Omnibus Vol. 14	0-312-33534-2	$11.95/$14.95 Can.
Sunday Omnibus Vol. 8	0-312-32440-5	$11.95/$14.95 Can.
Sunday Omnibus Vol. 7	0-312-30950-3	$11.95/$14.95 Can.
Sunday Omnibus Vol. 6	0-312-28913-8	$11.95/$14.95 Can.

Variety Puzzles

Acrostic Puzzles Vol. 10	0-312-34853-3	$9.95/$11.95 Can.
Acrostic Puzzles Vol. 9	0-312-30949-X	$9.95/$11.95 Can.
Sunday Variety Puzzles	0-312-30059-X	$9.95/$11.95 Can.

Previous volumes also available

Portable Size Format

Expand Your Mind Crosswords	0-312-36553-5	$6.95/$8.50 Can.
After Dinner Crosswords	0-312-36559-4	$6.95/$8.50 Can.
Crosswords in the Sun	0-312-36555-1	$6.95/$8.50 Can.
Will Shortz Presents Crosswords To Go	0-312-36694-9	$9.95/$11.95 Can.
Favorite Day Crosswords: Monday	0-312-36556-X	$6.95/$8.50 Can.
Piece of Cake Crosswords	0-312-36124-6	$6.95/$8.50 Can.
Carefree Crosswords	0-312-36102-5	$6.95/$8.50 Can.
Groovy Crosswords from the '60s	0-312-36103-3	$6.95/$8.50 Can.
Little Black (and White) Book of Crosswords	0-312-36105-X	$12.95/$15.95 Can.
Will Shortz Present Crosswords for 365 Days	0-312-36121-1	$9.95/$11.95 Can.
Easy Crossword Puzzles for Lazy Hazy Crazy Days	0-312-35671-4	$6.95/$8.50 Can.
Backyard Crossword Puzzles	0-312-35668-4	$6.95/$8.50 Can.
Fast and Easy Crossword Puzzles	0-312-35629-3	$6.95/$8.50 Can.
Crosswords for Your Lunch Hour	0-312-34857-6	$6.95/$8.50 Can.
Café Crosswords	0-312-34854-1	$6.95/$8.50 Can.
Easy as Pie Crosswords	0-312-34331-0	$6.95/$8.50 Can.
More Quick Crosswords	0-312-34246-2	$6.95/$8.50 Can.
Crosswords to Soothe Your Soul	0-312-34244-6	$6.95/$8.50 Can.
Beach Blanket Crosswords	0-312-34250-0	$6.95/$8.50 Can.
Simply Sunday Crosswords	0-312-34243-8	$6.95/$8.50 Can.
Crosswords for a Rainy Day	0-312-33952-6	$6.95/$8.50 Can.
Crosswords for Stress Relief	0-312-33953-4	$6.95/$8.50 Can.
Crosswords to Beat the Clock	0-312-33954-2	$6.95/$8.50 Can.
Quick Crosswords	0-312-33114-2	$6.95/$8.50 Can.
More Sun, Sand and Crosswords	0-312-33112-6	$6.95/$8.50 Can.
Planes, Trains and Crosswords	0-312-33113-4	$6.95/$8.50 Can.
Cup of Tea and Crosswords	0-312-32435-9	$6.95/$8.50 Can.

Other volumes also available

For Young Solvers

New York Times on the Web Crosswords for Teens	0-312-28911-1	$6.95/$8.50 Can.
Outrageous Crossword Puzzles and Word Games for Kids	0-312-28915-1	$6.95/$8.50 Can.
More Outrageous Crossword Puzzles for Kids	0-312-30062-X	$6.95/$8.50 Can.

St. Martin's Griffin